KITTY

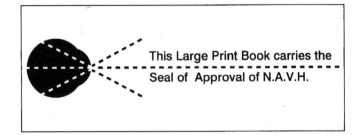

MARION CHESNEY

KITTY

Thorndike Press • Waterville, Maine

Published in 2002 by arrangement with
Lowenstein Associates, Inc.

Thorndike Press Large Print Candlelight Series.

The tree indicium is a trademark of Thorndike Press.

The text of this Large Print edition is unabridged.
Other aspects of the book may vary from the original edition.

Set in 16 pt. Plantin.

Printed in the United States on permanent paper.

Library of Congress Cataloging-in-Publication Data

Chesney, Marion.
    Kitty / Marion Chesney.
      p. cm.
    ISBN 0-7862-3625-6 (lg. print : hc : alk. paper)
    1. Large type books. I. Title.
PR6053.H4535 K68 2002
  823′.914—dc21   2001053426

KITTY

Chapter One

The sound of the church bells vibrated in the icy air of the bedroom as Kitty struggled awake. She lay burrowed beneath the bedclothes, staring at the frost flowers on the window, and wishing in a most unchristianlike way that it would turn out to be any day other than Sunday.

Sunday meant church service at St. John's, standing in the snow on the porch after the service, writhing under the patronizing remarks of Lady Worthing and her daughters while her mama smiled and simpered. Sunday was also Mama's "visit to the poor" day where, in her turn, she could enjoy her weekly luxury of patronizing her social inferiors. Sunday meant a heavy stolid meal under the glare of her taciturn stockbroker father and then back out into the cold again for evening service.

With a sigh, she threw back the bedclothes and scurried, shivering, to crack the ice on her pitcher of washing water on the stand. Her little white face overshadowed by an enormous pair of gray eyes, stared back at her from the looking glass over the washstand. Kitty struggled into her camisole and stays, shivering at the bite of the icy whalebone against her body. She pulled on her cotton stockings, twisting them slightly to hide the darns at the heel. Now the one good silk dress, smelling of benzine from overfrequent cleaning. It was of an uncompromising shade of brown with plain tight sleeves and a simple skirt.

How poor Kitty longed for warm, pretty, and feminine clothes!

She brushed her fine brown hair till it crackled down to her waist. If only she could wear it up. But mama said she must not put it up until her coming-out, but how and where she was to come out was a mystery since the Harrisons were obviously in very straightened circumstances.

The house on the edge of Hampstead Heath in North London was of elegant proportions, but the heavy Victorian furniture was old and worn and the curtains and carpets, threadbare. Unlike their wealthier neighbors, the Harrisons only kept a small staff, one general cook-housekeeper, one parlor maid, and a "daily" to do the heavy work.

Mrs. Harrison was already fussing

around the dining room when Kitty made her entrance. She was a thin, angular woman with peculiarly light, colorless eyes. Her heavy iron-gray hair was swept up on top of her head and anchored in place by a battery of ferocious steel pins which were forever escaping from their moorings and rattling to the floor. She wore a long tweed jacket and skirt, more suited to the winter's day than Kitty's best silk.

The meager breakfast was spread among a selection of tarnished silver dishes on the sideboard. Selecting two pieces of kidney and a thin sliver of toast, Mrs. Harrison turned to her shivering daughter. "I do wish we could persuade Mr. Harrison to let you have a length of wool for a winter dress, my dear. But as it is, I am afraid you must wear your silk. We must always remember to keep up appearances in front of Lady Worthing for, although we cannot aspire to her level of society and must always know our place, I know she appreciates our efforts to be always well-dressed."

Kitty edged toward the tiny fire in the grate that seemed unable to combat the stuffy cold of the overfurnished room with its heavy marble nudes — bought at an auction at Jobson's in a rare extravagant mood by Mr. Harrison — the heavy red, plush chairs, the draped mantel crowded with photographs and ancient seaside shell mementos, the dining table swathed in three heavy cloths and the massive, threadbare velvet curtains with their dingy bobbles framing the winter's scene of the Heath. Various oil paintings in need of cleaning decorated the walls with their massive gilt frames. Hot and airless in summer and cold and suffocating in winter, it seemed a fitting room for the massive, heavy Harrison meals of cuts of cheap meat and tired vegetables bought for a few pence at the end of the day, in the stalls of Camden Town market.

Mrs. Harrison was wont to bemoan the fact that no amount of solid feeding would plump out Kitty's delicate, slim figure into the rounded hour-glass mold which was *so* fashionable. Mrs. Harrison had long put away dreams of getting a foot into high society by means of a dazzling marriage for her daughter. In her eyes, Kitty was plain and depressingly timid. The fact that her own overbearing personality had brought about the latter fault never once occurred to her and the more shy Kitty became, the more raucous and bullying her mother grew.

With a martyred sigh, she finished her breakfast. "Come along, Kitty. Don't dawdle. Have you got your Bible? Now do remember to smile when Lady Worthing addresses you. It is a most important connection for me." She hustled Kitty before her and out into the hallway, past the study door where her father sat alone with his mysterious accounts, and then into the freezing air of the winter's day.

The frozen trees on the Heath stood mournfully under their coating of hoar frost and raised their twisted limbs up to the leaden sky as if praying hopelessly for spring.

Mrs. Harrison hurried up the icy road pushing Kitty in front of her like an angry mother hen with a recalcitrant chick. Kitty's long tweed cape was insufficient to keep out the bite of the wind, sweeping over the frozen ponds on the Heath from Highgate. The way other people dreamt of riches or power, Kitty dreamt simply of warmth. Only listening with half an ear to her mother's complaining monologue, she conjured up visions of enormous blazing fires burning merrily in bright uncluttered rooms.

"Kitty, you are *not* attending."

"Yes, Mama. The housekeeper . . ."

11

"Exactly. It is a disgrace. Mrs. Bennet wants 70 pounds a year. Ridiculous, I told her. Servants these days are getting so uppity. I told her there were only three of us to care for and . . ."

Kitty went back to warm her hands at her dream fire. Cook-housekeepers came and went — each one more slovenly than the last. Mrs. Harrison always referred to each new addition as "our old retainer."

"I would turn her off tomorrow but one must look after old servants," unaware that everyone knew that the old retainer had been with them only a few months.

At last they reached the church. Kitty waved to several of her old schoolfriends and got a lecture from her mother. "You must cut these connections, Kitty. Not at all the thing. Miss Bates's seminary may have been excellent for the money, but do remember these are the daughters of *shopkeepers*. You must try to get more elegant connections."

Kitty bowed her head and followed her mother into the church. The familiar Anglican smell of oil heaters, damp prayer books, and incense greeted her. With a sinking heart, she noticed that Lady Worthing was already ensconced in her pew with her two daughters, Ann and

Betty. As usual, she was unseasonably hatted. Her puglike face stared round the church from the shadow of a broad-brimmed straw hat that was topped up with a plethora of shiny, hard, wax fruit. The dead skins of several small ferrety animals hung around her ample bosom, their glass eyes gazing fixedly at the congregation in a ludicrous parody of their owner's stare.

The Reverend James Ponsonby-Smythe was reading from the Old Testament and the passage he had selected seemed entirely composed of who begat whom. Kitty sat on in an agony of boredom. Her despised friends were giggling and whispering and passing each other notes. "What fun it would be to be part of it all," thought poor Kitty. "Must I always be condemned to live in this sort of social isolation — neither belonging to the one class or the other?"

There was a sudden stir at the back of the church. Heads began to turn and even Lady Worthing's glassy eyes lit up with a sort of unholy glee. Kitty was about to risk a parental rebuke and turn and stare, when she noticed that her mother was twisted round in the pew, blatantly staring herself.

The object of all this attention was standing at the back of the church, leaning languidly on his cane. Her first impression of him was that he was extremely handsome. Her second, that he had one of the cruelest and most decadent faces she had seen outside the covers of a history book. Above his long, frogged, beaver coat, his face stood out against the dimness of the church with the translucent whiteness of alabaster. His hooded eyes surveyed the suburban congregation with weary contempt. His black, luxuriant curls were worn slightly longer than the common fashion and in his long white fingers, he carried a pair of lavender gloves. Suddenly, Kitty realized that he was looking straight at her. A mocking light flashed across his pale gray eyes, and he unmistakably winked.

"Well, really," said Kitty's mother, bridling. "Turn round this instant, miss. That man is nothing but a — a — *masher.*"

Kitty dutifully turned around. Secretly she was pleased. Mrs. Harrison had dinned into Kitty day and night about how plain she was and how undistinguished. It was nice to get a tiny bit of attention from one of that mysterious opposite sex.

As they rose to leave the church, Mrs.

Harrison drew Kitty close to her to prevent the "masher" from making any further overtures and then stopped on the church porch with a cluck of dismay, for there was that very gentleman being positively beamed upon by Lady Worthing. Kitty tried not to giggle. Lady Worthing was presenting one daughter after another to the gentleman, in feverish rotation. "This is my little Betty. And this is dear Ann. Did I introduce Betty? Now you must meet Ann. Betty have you . . ."

She broke off with a frown as she saw Mrs. Harrison approaching and gave a small, imperious wave of her plump hand encased in a dog-skin glove, in an attempt to dismiss the approaching distraction. But Mrs. Harrison was made of sterner stuff.

"My dear Lady Worthing," gushed Mrs. Harrison, sailing forward as majestically as King Edward's yacht at Cowes. "I was just saying to Kitty this morning — was I not, Kitty? — that if my dear Lady Worthing is not in church then somehow Sunday will just not be Sunday."

"Indeed," said Lady Worthing, reluctantly giving Mrs. Harrison two fingers to shake. She then turned her broad back to screen Mrs. Harrison from the gentleman,

15

but he demanded in a lazy drawl, "Aren't you going to introduce me, Lady Worthing?"

Lady Worthing turned slowly, her protruding eyes holding an expression which boded ill for Mrs. Harrison's future social ambitions. "Mrs. Harrison — Lord Chesworth — Lord Chesworth — Mrs. Harrison." His lordship gave a slight bow and turned his eyes questioningly at Kitty. "Oh, er . . ." humphed Lady Worthing, "this is her daughter, Kitty. Now as I was saying. . . ." She again presented her back to the Harrisons, but Mrs. Harrison nipped around her and faced Lord Chesworth, smiling and fluttering. "What brings you to our Hampstead church, Lord Chesworth?" gushed Mrs. Harrison while her mind deftly flicked the pages of the peerage. She had got it! Lord Peter Chesworth, third Baron Reamington. Unmarried!

"I was passing," said Lord Chesworth, "and felt in need of spiritual guidance." His eyes raked over Kitty with near insolence, taking in the shabby tweed coat and depressing felt hat. Kitty was suddenly aware of the darns in her gloves and pulled down her sleeves with a jerk.

Lady Worthing laughed indulgently. "We

have a nice little congregation here. Smells a bit of the shop but worthy people for all that."

Again the mocking gleam came into Lord Chesworth's eyes. "I met your late husband a few years ago, Lady Worthing. He gave me a very interesting lecture on the cotton mills of Lancashire."

Lady Worthing flushed an unlovely shade of red. Sir Jacob Worthing had made his money out of his mills and some unkind people had said that he had bought his knighthood. Since his death the previous year, Lady Worthing had lived with the polite fiction that their money came from "[their] estates in the north."

Small, powdery flakes of snow were beginning to fall from the leaden sky. Kitty shivered.

"We shall all catch pneumonia if we stand here chatting," said his lordship. "Good day to you, ladies." With that, his tall figure strode off.

The ladies watched him mount into a high-sprung brougham outside the church-yard gate. The coachman cracked his whip, the footman sprang up behind, and the party watched in silence until the erect figure of Lord Chesworth had disappeared around the corner.

17

Lady Worthing turned to Mrs. Harrison with a look of undisguised venom. "I never thought that you would be so encroaching, Mrs. Harrison. We have often talked about various types not knowing their place." And before Mrs. Harrison could reply, she swung her small animals around her thick neck, marshalled her two insipid daughters in front of her, and marched to her carriage.

It was Mrs. Harrison's darkest hour. Lady Worthing's voice had carried around the churchyard. She had been humiliated in front of the very people she despised. Two spots of color burned on her thin, yellowish cheeks and in some obscure way, she felt the fault was Kitty's.

"This would never have happened," she snapped, "if you had not been making sheep's eyes at his lordship in church."

"But I didn't, Mama," cried Kitty.

"Nonsense. Of course you did. A gentleman like that would not take notice of a little girl like you, otherwise. You're bold, Kitty, that's what you are."

"You said he was a masher," said Kitty, feeling for the first time a small spark of rebellion.

"How dare you answer me back!" said Mrs. Harrison, taking Kitty's arm in a

18

painful grip. "That was before I knew he was a Baron!"

Luncheon was a gloomy affair. Cold mutton followed by cold ham followed by cold pudding. Mrs. Harrison had tried to persuade the servants to serve hot food on Sundays, as they now did in the more fashionable households, but her small staff were underpaid and knew it. Although they were afraid of Mrs. Harrison's bullying manner, they knew to an inch what they could get away with. And so unfashionable, cold food lay untouched in front of Mrs. Harrison's jaundiced eye. She tried to tell her husband of her woes, but Mr. Harrison retreated to his study with his usual rejoinder, "Wish you had more money, don't you. Well, you ain't getting any."

Kitty suddenly remembered a summer's day when she was ten years old and her father had taken her to Southend. What a jolly, affectionate father he had been then! How the sun had shone and the water had sparkled and the band had played. There had been another lady there, very young and pretty, who had enjoyed the day as much as Kitty. But by evening, her father and the lady had had some kind of disagreement and ever since, he had become the taciturn, withdrawn man, she knew now.

Sometimes on Wednesday evenings there was the spark of the old Frederick Harrison. He always went out on Wednesday evenings without fail, resplendent in the glory of two waistcoats and a ruby pin and returned long after Kitty had gone to bed. Once, when she had crept down in the early hours of Thursday morning to get a glass of milk from the kitchen, she had met him coming home. He had been standing in the doorway of the hall, swaying slightly. He had looked at her in surprise as if he had never seen her before and suddenly taken an orchid out of his buttonhole and handed it to her. As she had stood there in amazement, looking at the beautiful flower, he had rapped out harshly, "Well. What y' standing there for. Get to bed."

Fine snow was beginning to pile up on the window ledges of the dining room. "Perhaps we should not go to Camden Town today, Mama," ventured Kitty. But Mrs. Harrison was still smarting from Lady Worthing's snub and the only way to heal the wound was to enjoy her usual Sunday pastime.

"I am so very cold, Mama," said Kitty. "Can't I put on something warmer?"

"Certainly not," snapped Mrs. Harrison. "We must always look our best before our social inferiors."

Kitty sighed as she thought of another Sunday afternoon with the poor Pugsleys, who lived in a crowded tenement in Camden Town, and who always seemed to have another baby.

At least I will be warm, she thought, as she marched behind her mother carrying a heavy earthenware pot of soup. People like the Pugsleys knew how to keep warm in winter even if they had to burn the furniture.

By the time Mrs. Harrison had delivered herself of her usual homily on the disease of poverty and the Pugsleys had accepted the soup with all the necessary resentful gratitude, it was growing dark. In an unexpected fit of generosity, Mrs. Harrison took a hansom home and warmed herself considerably with a spirited altercation with the cabby who wanted a whole shilling.

As Kitty went to bed that night, she was haunted by a thin white face and drooping eyelids. Well, she would dream about him and pretend that he was her Prince Charming. Goodness knows, there was no one else.

By Monday morning, the light snow had stopped falling and left enough to be uncomfortable and not enough to be dramatic. Mr. Harrison departed for the city and Mrs. Harrison, thinking that perhaps her daughter had charms that she had failed to perceive, sent her off to the drapers in the high street to buy brown-velvet ribbons to embellish that Sunday silk dress.

The draper's son, John Stokes, was busy stacking up bales of cloth as Kitty entered the dark shop. She was the only customer.

John Stokes was a plump young man with a penchant for tight clothes. Everything he wore was tight, his waistcoat, his trousers and his gloves. When he wore his hat on Sundays, even it was so tight, it left a red ring impressed on his chubby forehead. Although only two years older than Kitty, he liked to play man-of-the-world whenever she came into the shop.

"Do you know where I went last night, Kitty?"

Kitty shook her head shyly.

"Went to the music hall. I had the best time ever. What's say you come along with me one evening this week?"

"Oh, I couldn't," said Kitty much

alarmed. "Mama would never let me go anywhere unchaperoned and she would never, never let me go to a music hall."

"C'mon, Kitty. What about Wednesday night? You'll be safe with me. All you've got to do is say you're staying the evening at a friend's."

"I'm not allowed any friends," said Kitty bitterly. "Unless you count having Lady Worthing's daughters sneer at me."

"Why, that's it!" said John. "Say you're staying with Ann and Betty. Lady Worthing isn't going to speak to your mother again. We all heard her on Sunday. She'll gladly let you go and when Lady Worthing doesn't speak to her next Sunday, she'll just think she's gone cranky again. Let's go. You never get any fun. Think of it. All the music and lights and the people all dressed up."

The shop bell clanged and he turned away to serve the new customer, leaving Kitty with her thoughts. Somewhere in that other world of the heart of London was Lord Chesworth and, with the new Edwardian freedom, the aristocracy had been known to frequent music halls — even some of the ladies. John Stokes was a bit silly, but she had known him all her life and it would be just like going out with a brother.

Kitty stared out unseeingly at the snowy high street. The little spark of rebellion which had been there on Sunday grew to a small flame. This might be her only chance to have some fun. She took a deep breath and after the customer had left, said firmly, "Yes, John. I would like to go with you very much."

"That's the ticket," said John. "I'll pick you up in a hansom at eight. No! Not at the house. I'll wait down at the corner."

Kitty lived through each hour until Wednesday night in a fever of apprehension. Mrs. Harrison had delightedly swallowed the story, but to Kitty's horror, had bragged about her forthcoming visit to the Worthings to all and sundry. It was too late to retract.

At eight o'clock precisely on Wednesday evening, Kitty walked out into the London fog and with rapid steps made her way to the corner, where the hansom was waiting under a streetlamp. Inside was John Stokes, tightly clad as ever, resplendent in an embroidered waistcoat and a small diamond pin. He smelled overpoweringly of cologne and his hair gleamed with oil. He carried a silk opera hat on his chubby knees and was bubbling over with excitement.

When they descended from the hansom and into the full glare of the gaslight outside the music hall, John noticed his young companion's appearance for the first time. "Couldn't you have at least put your hair up, Kitty? You look like a schoolgirl."

Kitty replied with some spirit, "How could I, John? Mother would have known there was something up."

John gave her a sulky look. "Oh, very well, then. C'mon."

They entered the music hall and Kitty immediately wished she had not come. John led her to a table on the balcony and all around, in the glare of the gaslight, rose the raucous sound of male voices with their screeching female counterparts. "Time you got her home in bed," screamed the woman at the next table, pointing at Kitty, while the men with her all roared with laughter.

Kitty felt very self-conscious. Eyes seemed to be staring at her from every corner. Why? She could swear there were eyes boring into her back. She wriggled in the best silk dress, bravely embellished with velvet ribbons, and turned around to find herself looking straight into her father's flushed and furious face.

"Get out of here," he snarled.

"But I've paid for the tickets," bleated poor John.

"Get out!" screamed Mr. Harrison, raising his fist as if to strike. "I'll deal with you, Kitty, when I get home."

The sorry pair made their way back out into the shivering fog. No cabby seemed to want to go to Hampstead and when they at last got one who said he would take them for double fare, John was too weary to argue.

In sulky silence he left Kitty at the corner of the road and, with a heavy heart, she returned home to parry her mother's avid questions about her evening with the Worthings. Kitty knew at that minute she should confess all, but her small stock of courage had run out. She finally escaped to her room and lay staring at the ceiling with frightened, sightless eyes, waiting for the sounds of her father coming home. What on earth had her staid father been doing at a music hall? Perhaps he had been entertaining some of those business associates he always talked about.

In the early hours of the morning she heard a heavy pounding at the street door. Frightened, she ran to the head of the stairs in time to see her mother going to answer it. As the servants would have said, their wages were not enough to make them want to get out of bed on a winter's night.

A policeman stood there with his heavy helmet under his arm.

As in a dream, Kitty heard his voice. "Mrs. Harrison? There's been sort of an accident, mum. Well, that is, Mr. Harrison . . . he's dead."

Chapter Two

The house of mourning lay shrouded in wait for the funeral. It seemed to Kitty as if winter himself had decided to move in. Everything was as cold and hushed and silent as the day outside. White-faced and grim, Mrs. Harrison moved about the rooms, bemoaning the cost of the mourning clothes, the price of the funeral meats, and the moneyless future ahead.

"He always said we had no money in the bank," moaned Mrs. Harrison. "Thank goodness he had the foresight to pay for his own funeral."

Before the cortège moved off to Highgate Cemetery, a brougham carrying four very expensively dressed men arrived. They had come to pay their last respects to "old Fred." Kitty recognized them as being the men who were with her father that night at the music hall, but thankfully they did not seem to recognize her.

Frederick Harrison had dropped dead of a heart attack outside the music hall. "He must have been passing. I mean he would never have gone anywhere like that," said Mrs. Harrison.

At the subdued funeral banquet, Kitty heard one of the men exclaim to her mother, "Surprised to see old Fred lived in such a style. Always thought he was a warm man." But Mrs. Harrison took it as a compliment and wished heartily that the guests would leave so that the lawyer could read the will. Lady Worthing had not deigned to appear, to Kitty's relief and Mrs. Harrison's eternal disappointment.

Finally, the last black-gloved and black-hatted figure had disappeared and the lawyer had arrived and was closeted with Mrs. Harrison in the study. Kitty sat at the foot of the stairs, a pale, frail figure in her new black dress, and reflected that it was ironic indeed that her father had to die before she could get a new dress. She could not really mourn the brusque, unfeeling man she had never really known, so she thought instead of her father as he had been on that glorious day at Southend and forgot the years in between.

A scream from the study made her head jerk up. They must be ruined indeed. She scratched timidly at the door but only got a furious shout of "go away" from her mother. She returned to her seat on the stairs.

At last the lawyer left and her mother called her into the once-forbidden territory of her father's study. Mrs. Harrison's eyes burned with an unnatural glitter and her hands were shaking.

"Sit down, Kitty," she said in a deceptively mild voice. She indicated a high-backed, red-velvet chair and as Kitty sat down primly on the edge, she pulled another chair close until their knees were nearly touching and taking a deep breath, she began.

"Mr. Harrison's lawyer has just read me his will in which he leaves everything to me. Everything! And we are rich, Kitty. Very rich. Rich in stocks and bonds and property. Rich enough to take our rightful place in society."

Her voice took on a harder tone. "Mr. Harrison expressed the wish in his will that we should live as thriftily as always." Her thin bosom swelled and the edges of her corset stood out sharply against her mourning black silk.

"Pah!" Kitty recoiled as her mother spat full on the papers on the desk. "Thriftily indeed! The old miser. Well, may he turn in his grave but we are going into society and *you* my dear are going to marry a title.

We shall have a house in the West End and the best of everything and may Lady Worthing *rot* in the suburbs till she dies."

Mrs. Harrison's hairpins rattled on the worn linoleum as she jabbed her head backward and forward in excitement. Her pale eyes burned with ambition.

"We shall have a carriage and — and — ladies' maids and gorgeous gowns and —"

Kitty was frightened. "Couldn't we wait in Hampstead a little bit longer," she interrupted, "just to get used to the idea?"

"I am already used to poverty," snapped Mrs. Harrison. "I do not intend to endure slovenly servants, cold rooms, and bad food for a minute longer than need be. I should have known you would snivel in that cowardly way of yours. Just remember, my girl, after all the sacrifices I have made for you, I intend to see you well-married as my reward.

"And you will marry the man I choose."

Kitty bowed her head. The flame of rebellion flared up and died. Her mother sat staring into space, her lips moving soundlessly, as Kitty backed slowly from the room.

She desperately felt the need of a friend to talk to. Hetty Carson had been her close friend at school, but, as Hetty's father ran

31

the local bakery, Mrs. Harrison had cut the "undesirable connection."

Coming to a decision, she put on her coat and hat and started to walk down the hill to the Carson home in Gospel Oak. A wild wind was rioting over the Heath as if blown in from some faraway summer country. Puddles were forming in the hard crust of snow and flocks of rooks wheeled and danced under the rushing clouds. Two children ran past her down the hill, bowling their metal hoops in front of them and leaving thin tracks in the slush. Another party of youngsters were sledging on the Heath. They all piled up in a heap at the bottom and fell into the wet snow, roaring and laughing, oblivious of the damage to their clothes. Kitty tried to imagine a household where children were allowed to arrive home wet and muddy, but failed.

The Carsons' trim, two-storied terrace house was ablaze with light in the darkening evening. Hetty herself answered the door and looked in amazement at her old schoolfriend.

"Why, Kitty!" she exclaimed. "What is the matter, you poor thing? Your papa was buried just today. What are you doing here?"

"Please let me in, Hetty," said Kitty. "I've got to talk to someone."

Hetty led the way into a little parlor in the front of the house where a fire was blazing cheerfully and refused to let her friend speak until the tea tray with its load of pastries from the bakery had been brought in.

She was a plump, pretty girl with masses of shiny brown ringlets and a perpetual air of surprise in her wide, blue eyes.

As Kitty unfolded her tale of how the Harrisons were going to be rich and live in the West End, a flicker of jealousy darted across Hetty's eyes.

"Honestly, Kitty. The things you complain about. I swear if you'd been told you had no money at all, you would have been happier."

Kitty desperately tried to catch her old friend's sympathy. "But Mama says I've got to marry the man she chooses for me."

Hetty looked at the frail, delicate figure with some irritation. "With your mama's ambitions, she's likely to find you an earl or a lord. Why, you're the luckiest girl in Hampstead."

Kitty sighed and began to collect her handbag and gloves, preparatory to leaving. Hetty obviously thought she was a fool.

But Hetty was shrewd. If little Kitty Harrison was moving up to the West End, she had better hang on to the friendship. Hetty put her arms around the girl.

"I see I haven't really understood what's bothering you, dear. Tell me about it all over again."

Kitty hesitated but the unaccustomed sympathy was too much for her. She took Hetty, step by step, through the events leading up to the reading of the will; her fears for the future, her dreams about Lord Chesworth, and meeting him in the church.

Hetty gasped and exclaimed appreciatively and Kitty felt soothed and at home. As she left, she hugged her friend. "I'll never forget you, Hetty. I'll always know I have one real friend."

Hetty smiled mistily and pressed her hand warmly. But as the door closed behind Kitty's slim back, Hetty muttered to herself, "And don't you forget it, Miss Kitty Harrison. I'm going to need *you* one day."

Kitty hastened toward home. The streetlamps were already lit and the freakish summer wind had fled the Heath leaving it still, white, and frozen, the slush lying in hard-packed, ankle-breaking ruts.

There was a dark little shop next to Carson's bakery which contained a fascinating jumble of the flotsam and jetsam of the recently-fled Victorian age. The shop was closed, but in the blazing light from the bakery next door, Kitty could make out the objects in the window. Various mementos of the Crystal Palace Exhibition rubbed shoulders with wax fruit entombed in cracked-glass cases. Heavy pinchbeck and paste jewelry winked in the light from the baker's and a moth-eaten stuffed owl gazed out at the winter Heath with his huge glass eyes.

In the center of the window was a picture. It was of two young children, a boy and a girl, running through a meadow of waving, green grass and poppies. The boy was laughing and waving his sailor hat in the air and the little girl was turning to look down at a Scottie dog that was tugging at the edge of her small crinoline dress. Behind them ran a young nurse, the streamers of her starched cap flying in the painted wind and beyond the sunny meadow peeked the roofs of a thatched cottage. To Kitty it represented the very essence of magical childhood. Peering closer, she could see a small price tag in the corner. Five shillings. She simply must have that picture. Surely now that they were so rich, five shillings was a mere trifle.

She broached the matter at dinner, expecting a rebuff, but Mrs. Harrison was trying to break the habits of twenty-five married years of parsimony and gave her a whole pound note for herself. Not only that, she smiled — actually smiled — as she handed it over.

Kitty went up to her room in a happy daze to find another surprise. A fire was blazing merrily on the hearth and the scuttle beside it was topped up with a generous supply of coals. Feeling dimly that it was wrong to be so comfortable on the day of her father's funeral, Kitty went to bed. She would not have been so happy had she known the plans in her mother's head.

Mrs. Harrison was shrewd enough to know that money alone would not allow her into the hallowed circles of top Society. She would need a sponsor — some impoverished female of impeccable background. Without consulting any of her local acquaintances who would have considered it vulgar and indecent on the day of her husband's funeral, she had gone to the offices of the *Times* and had had an advertisement inserted in the personal column. She would await the results of that, before making her next move.

Making sure the curtains were tightly drawn, she picked up a bottle of her husband's best brandy and poured herself a generous goblet and, with a pleasurable feeling of sin, threw an enormous shovel of coal on the already blazing fire.

The next week produced a surprising number of replies to Mrs. Harrison's advertisement. With a gimlet eye on *Burke's Peerage*, she vetted every name until she came to that of Lady Amelia Henley. Lady Henley was the wife of the late Sir George Henley, a Tory M.P. of apoplectic disposition, who had died the previous year at the opening day of Ascot races. Mrs. Harrison remembered the gossip at the time in the newspapers and subsequent mention of Lady Henley at various society events. She was sure this was an answer to her prayers and, with a trembling hand, penned a letter to Lady Henley asking her to call.

At the time fixed, a hansom deposited Lady Henley outside the Harrison home. Mrs. Harrison took gleeful note of the hansom from behind the lace curtains of the parlor window. So Lady Henley had no private carriage!

Lady Henley stood on the pavement outside for a few seconds, surveying the house. She was a huge, massive woman encased from throat to heel in chinchilla. A pair of small black eyes surveyed the world from under the eaves of a black fur hat. She kicked open the gate with her smart buttoned boot and came lumbering slowly up the path like some rare species of bear.

Her first words of greeting were, as Mrs. Harrison was later to learn to her cost, entirely in character.

"Poky little place you've got here. You sure you've got money?"

Mrs. Harrison smiled sourly and ushered her into the parlor and then set about to impress Lady Henley with the exact magnitude of the Harrison fortune.

"Quite a tidy sum," said Lady Henley, stuffing a cream cake into her capacious mouth. "Well, do you want me or not?"

"It depends on your terms," replied Mrs. Harrison, hypnotized, as cake after cake disappeared into Lady Henley's maw. She gave the impression of inhaling pastry rather than eating it.

"My terms are this," she said indistinctly

through a barrier of cream sponge. "I've got this great house on Park Lane and I can't afford it. You take it over, servants and all, and I'll make sure you're presented everywhere. As for what you'll pay me — leave that to m'lawyer to settle. There's a girl y' say?"

"My daughter, Kitty," said Mrs. Harrison, ringing the bell. The parlormaid slouched in. "Lumley fetch Miss Kitty." Lumley stood for what seemed an age with her mouth open until the request was ponderously sorted out in her slow brain and slouched out again.

"An old retainer, you know," simpered Mrs. Harrison. She spoke to deaf ears. Lady Henley was bent over the cake stand. Contrary to custom, instead of starting with the thin cucumber sandwiches on the bottom and working her way up through the layers of buns and tea cakes and scones to the cream cakes at the top, Lady Henley had started eating the other way around. As Kitty entered the room, Lady Henley seemed surprised by the empty cake plate and moved her huge hand down to the fruitcake on the plate below.

She straightened up with a slice of cake halfway to her mouth and stared at the girl in the doorway. Kitty stood there, looking questioningly at Lady Henley, with her big gray eyes. Lady Henley felt a twinge of resentment. This stockbroker's daughter had a natural elegance, a natural breeding, which under the circumstances, she had no right to have. Lady Henley posted the cake into the mailbox of her mouth and reached for another tea cake, keeping her eyes fastened on Kitty.

"Lots of material there. But raw. Very raw. Needs polishing. Well, when I've finished with you, you'll marry a lord."

Mrs. Harrison hesitated. Could she endure living with this woman?

She addressed Lady Henley. "My name is Euphemia."

"What's that got to do with it?"

"Since we are to become friends, I shall call you 'Amelia' and you may call me 'Euphemia.' "

There was a silence as light colorless eyes met small black ones. Lady Henley recognized the steel in Mrs. Harrison's voice. After all, she heard it in the voices of her creditors nearly every day. "Euphemia," she said sourly.

The first hurdle was over.

"We met Lord Peter Chesworth at church one Sunday," said Mrs. Harrison. "I gather he is not married?"

"No," replied Lady Henley, her voice nearly drowning in Bath bun. "Furthermore, he's looking for a rich wife. Told me so the other day. He loves nothing but that great pile of his at Reamington. But it eats up the money and he's talking about taking out a mortgage."

"Indeed," said Mrs. Harrison with a sidelong glance at Kitty. "Indeed."

"I can get your daughter invitations to everywhere he goes during the season," said the remains of the Bath bun.

The next hurdle was over. Both middle-aged women stared at each other in silent agreement.

"Then I think we should discuss the matter of money in more detail before broaching it with our lawyers. Don't you agree . . . Amelia?"

Lady Henley looked at a cucumber sandwich and sighed. "Oh, all right."

Kitty was dismissed. She ran lightly up the stairs to her room to sit before her precious picture and dream of stepping through the frame into that happy, painted world.

Spring at last came to the Heath. The new grass turned and rolled in the sun all the way to Highgate. During the light evenings when the remains of winter hung on in the bluish hue at the end of the Hampstead streets and lanes, the faint sound of the German band playing in the tearooms at the Vale of Heath could be heard, jauntily banishing the middle-class night.

But the Harrisons' old home remained deserted with a few weedy daffodils blowing around the FOR SALE sign in the front garden. The Harrisons had taken up residence in Park Lane.

Kitty was preparing for her first ball. She had been kept out of sight until a truly massive wardrobe of clothes suitable for a debutante had been arranged. Lady Henley had ruthlessly instructed Mrs. Harrison to say that her husband had died the previous year. "Can't have the girl going about in black."

Kitty had often dreamt of getting ready for her first dance, and what she would wear, and how she would fix her hair. Until now, she had refused to let her French maid, Colette, dress her, but Colette had reported the fact to Lady Henley and Lady Henley and a huge plate of *petits fours* had assaulted the privacy of Kitty's bedroom to "put an end to such shopkeeper nonsense."

Poor Kitty! To have to stand naked in front of a supercilious French maid and endure the touch of her long, cold fingers, seemed humiliation indeed.

First her silk chemise was put on. Then the silk stockings were smoothed over her legs and clipped to the long, heavily-boned stays. Colette pulled the lacings round the waist with what seemed unnecessary savagery and then fastened pads on the hips and bust to achieve the hourglass effect. Then her drawers were hauled on, then her petticoat, and then the ball gown.

The ball gown was of simple white taffeta sweeping to a small train at the back and was cut lower on the bosom than most debutante dresses. But Lady Henley had crudely pointed out that if you wanted to sell the goods, you had to present them to their best advantage.

Her hair was piled up on her head over more pads and dressed with artificial flowers. A long fan with fringes was put in her hand, a string of pearls placed around her neck, and Kitty was ready to meet her new social contemporaries for the first time.

Lady Henley and her mother rose and stared at Kitty as she shyly entered the drawing room. Mrs. Harrison's eyes filled with sentimental tears. "Why, you look really pretty."

Lady Henley snorted and walked slowly around the girl, looking her up and down. "Not bad. Not bad at all," she commented finally. "But you need a bit of animation. Pour her a glass of sherry, Euphemia."

Mrs. Harrison moved stiffly across the room in all the glory of shot taffeta, a tremendous bustle and a new diamond necklace that she kept fingering nervously to make sure it was still there.

Lady Henley was encased in a purple silk dress of an old-fashioned cut showing a great deal of mottled bosom. A collar of large and dirty diamonds was clasped round the rolls of fat on her neck.

All three sat bolt upright with their drinks, restricted by their heavy stays. The drawing room, like the rest of the mansion in Park Lane, was light, charming, and characterless. Lady Henley had employed the services of an expert decorator and then imposed none of her heavy personality on the furnishings, unless you could count the trails of pastry crumbs that she left in her wake.

"Now remember, Kitty," she said. "We're going to a lot of expense to get you suitably married, so don't let us down."

"What about love. No one has mentioned love," said Kitty softly.

"Love! Pah!" said Lady Henley. "Love has no place in a high-society marriage. Have your fun afterwards if you want. There'll be plenty of chaps ready to oblige."

Kitty blushed and bit her lip. A conversation such as this could never have taken place in a middle-class drawing room.

Mrs. Harrison felt a strange pang of maternal anxiety. If only Kitty had some more spirit. She had a sudden wish that her biddable daughter would tell Lady Henley to go to hell. Then she stiffened her resolve. Such thoughts were mawkish. Once Kitty was married to Lord Peter Chesworth, she would be in the company of other young married women and then she would find that most of them had settled for money or a title. Romance was for novelists and shopkeepers.

"Isn't it time we left?" said Kitty looking at the clock. It was ten-thirty.

"We're going to make an entrance," said Lady Henley. "Make sure all the fellows get a good look at you."

Kitty's heart sank. She forced down her sherry and felt light-headed and slightly sick. Finally, Lady Henley rang for the carriage and they made their way out into the

April night. They bowled briskly along the London streets which seemed to be alive with all sorts of jolly, unfashionable people having a good time. The air was heavy with the scent of lilacs and lime. A young couple stood at a crossing, gazing into each other's eyes. Kitty looked away.

The ball was held at a mansion in Kensington. The hostess was a Mrs. Brotherton, a wealthy woman who had outlived her husband; it was an age when society women survived their spouses in great numbers.

The sound of a waltz drifted tantalizingly on the air as Kitty and her two formidable chaperones walked up the red carpet on the pavement, past the policeman on duty, and into the entrance hall. After leaving their cloaks, they mounted to the ballroom on the first floor. As they were late, their hostess had already joined the dance.

Kitty stood at the entrance watching the chattering, glittering, circling throng and tried to remember that they were only human beings. Various young men who all looked bewilderingly alike in black and white evening dress, white gloves and patent leather hair, wrote their names in her dance card. She stumbled her way dutifully round the dance floor, bewildered by the strange speech. Everything was "cheery" or "ripping," words she had not heard before. Finally, she was left to sit beside her mother. Then Lady Henley sailed up. "I must introduce you to a very good connection, Mrs. H— I mean, Euphemia." With a look in her eyes like a hunter closing in on his prey, Mrs. Harrison got to her feet with a protesting creak from her stays, and followed her massive friend.

Kitty sat on that uncomfortable piece of furniture called a rout chair and felt wretched. All the young people glittered and laughed and chatted around her as if she did not exist. She stared across the room and, for the second time, found herself looking straight into the eyes of Lord Peter Chesworth. He made every other man in the room look shoddy and insipid and very young. He moved slightly as if to cross to her side, but was waylaid by a dazzlingly smart lady dressed in scarlet chiffon. Long ruby earrings fell like drops of blood from her exquisite little ears and her black hair was piled on top of her head in glossy curls. Her eyes, which were of a light, clear blue with black lines round the irises, were gazing up at Lord Chesworth

47

in an intimate and tantalizing way. He took her arm and led her into the dance where she swayed against him, her tiny feet barely touching the floor.

The tiny spark of hope that the evening would turn out to be anything other than depressing, died in Kitty's heart as she watched them. She had spent her lonely hours building the Baron into a dream-lover because she had no other man to think of. She had heard that he was un-married. She had never considered that he would be attracted to anyone else. But there was worse to come.

"Have you met the new heiress, Kitty Harrison?" The voice seemed to be almost in her ear and she jumped. Leaning back in her chair, she realized that one of her dancing partners was on the other side of the pillar with a friend.

"Gawd, yes. Pretty little thing but she jumps all over one's feet and says 'beg pardon, beg pardon' the whole time, just like a bloody scullery maid."

His friend whispered something and the dancing partner popped his head around the pillar, saw Kitty, gave her a cheeky, un-repentant grin and moved off arm in arm with the other man.

Kitty sat on in misery, staring at the toe

of her dancing slipper. What was wrong with saying "beg pardon"? At Miss Bates's seminary it had been considered a very polite and ladylike thing to say.

The guests continued to circle under the orange glare of the recently installed electric lights. Not a very grand ball. At grand balls they used masses of candles, thought poor Kitty viciously, sitting surrounded by other wallflowers and the heavy scent of gardenias and wishing she were dead. No, that was not true. She wished *them* all dead first.

A shadow fell across her white dress and she looked up. Lord Chesworth was standing before her, flanked on either side by Lady Henley and Mrs. Harrison. He looked like a man who had just been arrested.

"May I have this dance, Miss Harrison?"

How Kitty longed for the courage to say no, rather than dance with a man who had obviously been coerced into it by her stern chaperones. She merely bowed her head and moved out onto the dance floor and, because she was past caring about anything, she danced beautifully. Lord Chesworth looked down at the silent girl and felt a twinge of pity which he immediately dismissed. The girl was obviously as pushing as her mother. Any girl who would sell herself into marriage for the sake of a title was not deserving of pity. Lady Henley had made it quite plain that Mrs. Harrison and her daughter were prepared to restore his estates for the sake of his title. A fair bargain.

He thought of Reamington Hall with affection. The spacious light rooms, the long driveway lined with magnificent lime trees, the pleasant park with its rolling lawns. If only he were there now instead of tied down in this stuffy, overheated room with this colorless girl.

Well, he must talk about something. He began to describe his home to her and, to his delight, found Kitty to be an enthusiastic audience. She knew nothing of the country. Hampstead Heath was about the nearest, she admitted with a shy laugh. Pleased and surprised, the Baron chatted on and surprised himself even further by taking her in for supper. He would marry the girl, he decided suddenly. She needed some social polish but she was malleable. Accordingly, when they returned to the ballroom, he left Kitty with her mother and returned to the supper room in search of Lady Henley.

She was tucked away at a corner table

Lady Henley was waiting for him in the morning room, sitting contemplating a plate containing six poached eggs, with great satisfaction.

"Trying to lose weight," she explained. "I always have a light breakfast."

Mrs. Harrison came fluttering in wearing an unfortunate choice of pastel-colored organza, which highlighted her yellowish complexion.

"Dear, dear, Peter. I may call you that mayn't I?" she gushed.

"Better let 'er," mumbled the poached eggs.

"Well, Peter. We have a lot to arrange. But first I would like to speak to you privately."

Lady Henley was about to protest but at that moment the butler entered bearing a fresh plate of toast, dripping with butter. She gave a primeval grunt and settled back in her chair.

In the study at the back of the house, Lord Chesworth politely waited for Mrs. Harrison to come to the point. In his short acquaintance with her, he would not have thought her shifty. But she moved about the room nervously, picking things up and putting them down. At last she said, "It's about Kitty. We are very honored by your

and the Baron watched her for a few minutes before joining her. After all, he thought, it was not every day he had the privilege of watching anyone eat smoked salmon and chocolate éclairs from the same plate.

The irony that this vulgar woman should be accepted everywhere while the refined and delicate Kitty was considered to lack "class," did not occur to him. This was the only world he knew and he would no more have questioned its taboos and shibboleths than he would have dreamt of selling Reamington Hall.

He sat down beside her and got right to the point. "I'll marry the girl."

"Good," said Lady Henley, wiping her fingers on her bosom. Traces of her progression through the dishes on the buffet were scattered through her diamond collar. A shred of Virginia ham clung to the top strand, a small piece of lettuce to the second, a sliver of quail bone pierced the third, and bits of éclair and smoked salmon were roosting on the bottom.

"She is willing to marry me?" questioned Lord Chesworth. "She seems such a biddable little thing."

"All to the good then," said Lady Henley, impaling a pickle. "Oh, she'll marry you right and tight. The only thing is — how much do I get out of it?"

"You don't," said Lord Chesworth, putting his thumbs in his waistcoat and leaning back in his chair. "Mrs. Harrison's already paying you to fix this. I know it and you know it, so don't get greedy."

Lady Henley shrugged and sent the debris of her repast flying about her skirts.

"Allonamurrerinamorden."

"What?" said Lord Chesworth, wondering if she was perhaps attempting to speak Swahili. Lady Henley spat out a mouthful of *canapés au parmesan*.

"I said, 'Call on her mother in the morning.'" Lord Chesworth felt that surely Kitty would consider anyone a relief after company such as this and took his leave. He had better get started right away and dance with Kitty again.

Outside the supper room his arm was caught by Mrs. Veronica Jackson, her red chiffon dress swirling in the evening breeze from the open windows around her perfect, hourglass figure.

"Peter! Why didn't you take me in to supper? It's not like you to dance attendance on schoolgirls."

"Well, I'm dancing attendance on this one," he said, straightening his waistcoat

with a jerk to cover his embarrassm
How could he tell this mistress of
years' happy liaison that he was abou
get married to someone else? He ha
ways parried her hints in that directio
persuading her that they were h
enough as they were and that he did
intend to get married at all.

As he crossed to Kitty's side,
Jackson watched him with an angry g
She was thirty-two years old and
beautiful. But, looking at Peter Chesw
dancing with Kitty, she began to fee
for the first time.

Kitty was in seventh heaven. The E
was not at all as cruel and supercilio
she had expected. He was charming
kind — and every other woman ir
room was jealous of her; Kitty was
nine and human enough to like that.

When her formidable escort finally
her home, she was in such a happy
that she allowed her maid to undres
without her usual shiver of distaste.

Lord Chesworth called prompt
eleven the next morning, resplenden
gray frock coat, biscuit-colored tro
and a yellow silk waistcoat embroi
with gold and scarlet hummingbirds.

proposal of marriage, but it suddenly seems all so mercenary."

"Of course it's mercenary," said Lord Chesworth. "You never tried to pretend it was anything else."

Mrs. Harrison's pins started to rattle to the floor, a sure sign of inner tumult. She said, "Kitty is such a young thing. It would be nice if you — if you — well, if you could pretend to be a little in love with her."

Lord Chesworth's gray eyes narrowed. "You mean the girl knows nothing of the arrangement?"

"Well, *of course,* she does. But young girls are romantic." Another hairpin fled the nest.

"I don't call it romantic to want gilt on the gingerbread in this situation," said the Baron roundly.

The softer emotions deserted Mrs. Harrison's bosom. The business gleam was back in her eye.

"I have agreed to restore your estates at no small cost, Peter. Surely this little thing is not too much to ask."

Peter Chesworth sighed. It was all so squalid but . . . there was Reamington Hall and it must be saved. In an unconscious imitation of Kitty, he bowed his head in assent.

Mrs. Harrison gave a grim smile. "I shall send her to you."

Kitty, who was enjoying the unaccustomed luxury of a long lie in bed, struggled awake as her mother erupted into the room and began dragging dress after dress from the wardrobe.

"Lord Chesworth is below, waiting to see you. I shall let him explain everything," said Mrs. Harrison, tugging at the bell rope to call Colette.

The two women thrust her into her stays and laced them so tight she could hardly breathe. Then a delicate Indian muslin was put on her slim figure and her brown hair was piled over the pads on the top of her head.

"Quickly, quickly," hissed Mrs. Harrison. Her hour of triumph was at hand and she did not wish the Baron to escape at the last minute.

She pushed Kitty ahead of her into the study and slammed the door on the happy couple. Mrs. Harrison stood in the hall for a moment, leaning her hot forehead against the cool wall. "And how's that, Frederick Harrison?" she muttered. "If you had been alive, you old miser, you would have had her married to the butcher's boy!"

She marched into the morning room. Lady Henley looked at her over a piece of toast. "Don't go leaving them alone too long," she commented. "Chesworth's got a bit of a reputation."

But in the privacy of the study, Lord Peter Chesworth was all that was correct. Clasping Kitty's trembling hand in his, he explained that he had fallen in love with her at first sight. He had to declare himself immediately before she was snatched up by someone else. Would she marry him?

Kitty looked up into his white, handsome, aristocratic face with her heart in her eyes. Would she? She would indeed. All her dreams had come true. She was marrying for love after all.

What a little actress, thought his lordship, gathering her into his arms.

He pressed his mouth to the fresh young lips in a chaste kiss and suddenly thought longingly of a pair of warm and fiery ones. What on earth was Veronica Jackson going to say to all this?

Mrs. Harrison opened the door and beamed on them. Ever correct, his lordship turned, holding Kitty by the hand. "Mrs. Harrison, your daughter has just done me the inestimable honor of accepting my hand in marriage."

After Lord Chesworth had left and she and Kitty and Lady Henley were sitting in the drawing room celebrating their triumph in their separate ways, the butler entered. "Lady Worthing and the Misses Worthing," he intoned.

Mrs. Harrison got to her feet and turned her back to the door.

"We are not at home."

There was an outraged gasp and the sound of retreating footsteps.

It was Mrs. Harrison's finest hour.

Chapter Three

Kitty sat down wearily after enduring the final fitting for her wedding dress and wished for the hundredth time that her fiancé were not quite so correct.

They were never alone. He had punctiliously escorted her to every society event — parties, operas, balls. Other engaged couples managed to spend some time alone together — on a balcony at a party, outside the box at the opera — there were endless opportunities. But not one of them did Lord Chesworth make use of.

Increasingly elegant and withdrawn, he chatted with her politely but never so much as kissed her glove. Arrangements were going ahead to furnish a pretty house in Green Street, but never once had her taste been consulted.

Then there was that time at the Royal Academy when she had entered one of the galleries with Lady Henley and seen him sitting on one of the benches with a lady whom he had introduced as Mrs. Veronica Jackson. Kitty recognized the lady of the red chiffon dress. Her blue eyes, amused and cynical, had raked Kitty from head to toe. "So that's your little bride, Peter!" she had commented lazily, keeping her primrose-gloved hand possessively on Lord Chesworth's. His lordship had simply given the lady an enigmatic look from under his hooded lids.

But they seemed to share some sort of secret, thought Kitty. Every pleasant ordinary thing they said to each other seemed to have a double meaning.

Well, he would change after they were married. And he had said he loved her. And Miss Bates had always said that a gentleman never lied.

London was in full summer bloom. Geraniums blazed in the window boxes and roses rioted in the gardens. The air was heavy with the scent of flowers. And in the evenings, the ballrooms and parties were so bedecked with great tubs of blooms that it was like stepping into a magnificent garden.

Kitty decided to forget her troubles and be "cheery." She rolled the new word round on her tongue and felt very dashing and modern.

If only she had some friends. She had been to various tea parties and "at homes" but, with the bear-like shadow of Lady Henley next to her, conversation seemed to be inhibited. The only people who came to call were old friends of Lady Henley. Surely these bright young people must have confidences and best friends, and Kitty, thinking of Hetty back in Hampstead, did long for a best friend.

The day of the wedding arrived at last. No expense had been spared. Mrs. Rosa Lewis's catering service had been hired and her staff of girls with their high, white, laced boots, white dresses, and chef's hats had taken over the kitchen.

Kitty stood in her bedroom, patiently raising her arms so that Colette could drop the white gown of Brussels lace over her head. The waist and the bodice were embellished with tiny seed pearls and the train was so long it required the attentions of six bearers. Even Lady Henley's forceful personality had not been enough to raise the necessary maids of honor and so the small children of various society families had been pressed into service.

A distant relative of Lady Henley, Mr. James Bennington-Cartwright-Browne, had been recruited to give the bride away. Kitty's timid suggestion that she might send an invitation to Hetty had been coldly received. "Ask the baker's daughter? Are you mad?" said Mrs. Harrison, dropping only one hairpin to show how minor the irritation was.

At last there was the church and there was the steeple, but who on earth were all these people? The pews seemed to be crowded with all of London's fashionable society and not a friendly face among the lot of them. They had come to see the Baron marry "his little shopgirl."

It was Veronica Jackson who had called Kitty that and society had delightedly taken up the phrase and exchanged story after gleeful story of Kitty's terribly middle-class "refeened" behavior. It made such good gossip that Kitty's quiet, well-bred manner was unable to contradict it. She was the latest joke in a season thin of jokes. So the shopgirl she remained.

It seemed as if it were all over so quickly. One minute she was Miss Kitty Harrison, the next she was Lady Kitty Chesworth, Baroness Reamington.

The reception was excellent, run with the firm hand of the famous Mrs. Lewis in the background. The aristocratic guests were obviously surprised, for they kept saying so in very loud voices.

Kitty waited patiently beside her new husband at the head of the long table. Would they never be able to leave? They were to spend their first night in their own town house and then travel to Reamington Hall on the following day. Kitty had secretly hoped to go somewhere exotic like Paris or Rome.

Her new husband seemed to be drinking a great deal of champagne in a quiet, steady manner. Mrs. Harrison was positively radiant; she would read about herself in the society columns at last! Lady Henley sat with her head sunk over her plate, for once absolutely stupefied with food.

The plover eggs served with cream cheese had been removed. That had been the eighteenth course, Kitty noted. Surely now it would end. But the last and nineteenth — *soufflées glacés à l'entente cordiale* and *bonbonnières de friandises* — was brought in and all the guests fell to cheerfully as if they were attacking the first. Then came the toasts. Kitty groaned inwardly. She had forgotten about them.

Mr. James Bennington-Cartwright-Browne was called upon to give the toast to the bride. But the gentleman had fallen sound asleep, his heavy, white, tobacco-stained moustache rising and falling gently and his freckled old hand stretched out to-ward his glass. His neighbor nudged him rudely and he came to life. "Eh, what? What, what?"

"Speech," hissed his neighbor.

"Oh, eh, harrumph. Just so." Mr. James Bennington-Cartwright-Browne lurched to his feet and surveyed the room with his rheumy eyes.

"I — ah — now — ah — declare this ba-zaar open." And amid cheers and hoots from the guests, he sat down and promptly fell asleep.

He was again nudged awake. "Toast to the bride," he was told.

"Eh, what bride?" said the old gentle-man. "The shop-gel, Kitty," hissed the woman on his other side. Once again Mr. James Bennington-Cartwright-Browne got to his feet. "Here's to the bride. Don't know 'er but I'm sure she'll do," he said and sat down again.

The shopgirl slur was not new to Kitty, but it was to her mother. Mrs. Harrison sat as if in a trance while the roar of conversa-tion swept around her ears like the un-heeding sea. "Shopgirl." For this, she had endured the gluttony of Lady Henley. For this, she had filled her house with these laughing, uncaring, and sneering people.

And — oh, bitter blow — for this she had sacrificed her daughter. Hairpins fell as thick as the leaves in Vallembrosa.

The best man was then called. He was a cheerful-looking young man with the uninspiring name of Percy Barlow-Smellie. A young matron across from Kitty leaned over and squeezed her arm. "You mustn't mind Percy. He's a terrible wag," she said.

Percy, after clowning around for several minutes pretending to have lost his speech, began.

"I couldn't think what to say, so I wrote a poem."

(Cheers. Good old Percy.)

"Here's to the wicked baron
Who didn't marry a harridan,"
(Loud laughter.)
"But he married Kitty,
Who is very pretty."
(Groans and hoots.)
"So now that we've got them wed
Let's get them into bed."
(Screams from the ladies. Applause from the men.)

Other speeches followed while Mrs. Harrison sat on as if turned to stone. These people would drink her wine and eat her food but never, never would they accept her.

The babble died down as Mrs. Harrison got to her feet and glared around the room.

"Get out," she said in a venomous whisper. Then her voice rose to a scream. "Get out, get out, get out!"

What a horrified rustling of lace and chiffon, satin and silk. Like a poultry yard after the fox had just broken in, the ladies rose in a flutter of feather boas and large feathered hats. The men stolidly got to their feet. Everyone paused. Mrs. Harrison *must* be drunk. They could not possibly have heard aright.

Suddenly, there was an upheaval near Mrs. Harrison. Like some huge primeval beast erupting from its swamp, Lady Henley rose from a litter of bones and crusts and crumbs.

"You heard 'er. Get out. Go on. Shoo!" And putting a pudgy arm round Mrs. Harrison's shoulders, she said, "C'mon, Euphemia. Let's get out of here."

The Baron turned to his new Baroness. "Well, Kitty. Shall we leave?"

Kitty gratefully took his arm. She simply wanted to get away. Everything would be all right as soon as she was alone with her new husband.

The younger wedding guests, their spirits restored, followed them, laughing and chattering, out to the carriage. The sun shone bravely while Kitty made her way shyly to the carriage through a rainstorm of rice and rose petals.

As Lord Chesworth took his place beside her, a group of young people led by a freckled-faced, tomboyish girl placed a large box tied up with ribbon on her lap. "It's from us — your new friends. You must open it *now*."

"Don't," said Peter Chesworth, laconically.

Kitty looked down at the circle of laughing faces and smiled shyly. She remembered Lady Henley's defense of her mother. They were not so bad after all.

She untied the pretty ribbons on the parcel, opened it — and screamed. A huge jack-in-the-box leapt out and hung wobbling in front of her, its mocking clown's face dancing before her tear-filled eyes.

"Drive on," snapped the Baron, and then turned to Kitty and held out his handkerchief. "You mustn't take everything so seriously. If you're ever going to feel comfortable in society, you must learn to take a joke."

In silence they entered the house in Green Street. Kitty was introduced to the staff who were lined up in the hall. The butler, a fat white man called Checkers, who seemed to have a perpetual cold, made a speech of welcome. Then the happy pair retired to the drawing room and surveyed each other in silence.

"Well, here we are," said Lord Chesworth crossing over to the looking glass and straightening his stock.

"Yes," whispered Kitty, wishing he would take her in his arms.

He turned around and looked at her with some irritation. "I'll stay here and have a drink. Why don't you go and see your rooms."

Kitty nodded and went up the stairs, noticing that the house seemed to be very dark. Burne-Jones stained-glass windows filtered the gloomy light down into the hall. Colette was waiting in the bedroom, unpacking the trunks.

She looked up as her mistress came in. "Well, you don't look much like a new bride," she commented.

Kitty felt this was an unpardonable piece of insolence, but had no spirit left to reply. She dismissed the maid and stretched out on the bed, staring at the ceiling, and wondering what the night would bring. At last she got to her feet and began to arrange her books on the shelves and a few of her photographs. She unwrapped her precious picture and looked around for a place to hang it. A heavy oil painting, depicting a group of damp, highland cattle looming through mist, hung on the wall facing the end of the bed. Kitty lifted it down and put it on the floor. She hung her painting carefully in its place. At least her new husband would see that she had some artistic taste.

Without ringing for Colette, she changed her dress and descended the stairs to look for her lord.

The house was empty and appeared deserted. A barrel organ was playing at the end of the street and the tinny music seemed to dance through the heavy silence. Timidly, she rang the bell.

Checkers informed her that his lordship had "stepped out." His watery eyes, sunken in wrinkled flesh, managed to convey that he considered this unsuitable behavior.

Kitty dismissed him and sat on the window seat, staring out into the twilight and longing for the courage to walk away from the house herself. Gradually her eyelids drooped and she fell asleep as the dusk gathered in the corners of the room.

She was awakened three hours later by the sound of the front door slamming and her husband's voice. "That's all right, Checkers. I shall be needing nothing further this evening." Then the door of the drawing room opened and he walked in.

His silk hat was placed at a rakish angle over his black curls and his eyes held a hectic gleam. He bent and kissed her full on the mouth. He smelled strongly of brandy.

"Why don't you run along and get ready for bed, my dear," said her new husband. "And I'll join you shortly."

Kitty looked at him with troubled eyes and then bent her head and left the room. What was she expected to do? If only she had had the courage to ask somebody.

Trailing her lace shawl behind her, she walked slowly upstairs to her bedroom. Was she to go to her bedroom or his? Well, he was in charge now and would surely let her know.

Colette had laid out a filmy nightdress on the bed. Kitty looked at it doubtfully and decided to wear one of her old flannel ones to give herself a feeling of comfort and protection. She slipped it on, buttoned it high at the throat, and climbed into bed where she sat upright, staring at the door.

After a few minutes it opened and her husband swaggered in. Kitty shrank back against the pillows and watched in dismay as he started to strip off his clothes in the full glare of the electric light. At last he stood naked, his slim, muscular body gleaming like polished marble. Kitty had not only never seen a naked man before, she hadn't the slightest idea of what one would look like.

Unaware of her distress, and more than a little tipsy, Peter Chesworth put one knee on the bed and prepared to climb in. His eye caught sight of Kitty's favorite picture on the wall and, with an exclamation, he went to take a closer look at it, standing with his hands on his hips, affording Kitty an excellent view of his naked back.

"Good God," he said slowly. "How on earth did that get there?"

"It's my favorite picture," said Kitty, with a trace of pride in her voice, despite her fright. "I bought it all by myself."

"So I should hope," he said, turning around. "For heaven's sake girl, didn't Lady Henley cure you of this penchant for chocolate-box art?"

It was the final straw. Her only piece of home, her darling picture, had been scorned by this grinning, naked satyr. She sank into the pillows and let out a whimper of pain.

Lord Chesworth was furious. "Stop acting. You don't think I'm going to go along with this little comedy, do you? I married you for your money. You married me for my title. And that's it. So stop squirming away there and let's make the best of the bargain."

Kitty couldn't believe her ears. "But you married me for love," she almost screamed, raising a tear-stained face from the pillow.

"Love?" said the Baron. "Oh, yes. I said all that when I asked you to marry me because your mama pointed out that you wanted gilt on your gingerbread. Love? There's about as much love in this game as there ever was in one of your late lamented father's business transactions."

Kitty began to cry in earnest, great, dry, racking sobs. The Baron was unmoved. He started putting on his clothes at full speed.

"Your type never could take honesty." He turned in the doorway. "Why, you're nothing but a spoiled brat."

He marched off down the stairs and, a minute later, Kitty heard the street door slam. She cried until she could cry no more. It could not be true. He must have been drinking. She would ask her mother in the morning. With that, she fell into exhausted sleep, like a very young child.

Lord Chesworth had indeed been drinking and was in a black rage which was, from time to time, fanned by the unpleasant feeling that he had behaved like a cad. Well, he knew where to go for consolation. Shortly afterwards, he was ushered into Mrs. Jackson's bedroom and, without so much as a word, began taking off his clothes again.

Mrs. Jackson watched him triumphantly from her high, cane-backed bed. "On your wedding night, Peter? Is your little bride aware of what she is missing?"

He slid under the covers and held her close, his head beginning to reel with the effects of all he had drunk. "Miss Kitty expects love along with my title. Love! I swear to you, Veronica, if she were dead I would take her money and marry you without one pang of remorse." With that, he fell into a drunken stupor leaving his mistress to mull over his words, holding his head against her breast, and looking off into the distance with hard, calculating eyes. Then, she too, fell asleep.

Dawn blazed up over London and the early sun hung in the hot and already humid air. A blackbird sat on a tree outside Mrs. Jackson's bedroom window and poured his liquid song out over the dusty city streets. The Baron mumbled "Kitty," and groaned and turned over. He took one horrified look at Veronica Jackson's beautiful sleeping face and swung his legs over the edge of the bed and buried his feverish forehead in his hands.

Yesterday came back to him through a gray fog of memory, interspersed with bright flashes of total recall — Mrs. Harrison's angry face at the wedding, the jack-in-the-box, Kitty cowering and sobbing on the bed.

He groaned again, but softly this time, so as not to wake his sleeping partner. He must find out the truth. If Kitty really believed him to be in love with her, then he owed her a humble apology. But she must have been acting. She must.

He suddenly decided to go round to Park Lane and find out. He could not face Kitty again until he knew the truth.

With distaste, he climbed into the soiled clothes of the night before and decided to go to his club for a shave. He slipped from the room while Veronica slept on.

God, what a hangover! He winced in the brassy light and started to walk toward St. James's. Everything seemed unreal and still; a painful world filled with eye-hurting color. A bunch of roses in a crystal glass on someone's window ledge made him blink, and a line of scarlet geraniums seemed to positively swear at him from someone else's window box. He felt unreal and detached. A great black cloud of guilt hung somewhere on the horizon of his mind. A crossing sweeper tipped his can and grinned at the gentleman in his wedding clothes, showing all of his large, white teeth. To the Baron, his smile seemed to hang in the air, disembodied, like the Cheshire cat's grin. London was slowly coming to life. A cabby swerved to avoid him and swore loudly.

After being barbered at his club and having changed into a suit of clothes which he kept there for emergencies, he downed a large glass of brandy and port mixed together, prescribed by the steward, and felt better. Of course the girl had been acting! All the same, it would do no harm just to make absolutely sure. Tipping his hat jauntily to the side of his head and carrying his cane under his arm, he made his way toward Park Lane.

Mrs. Harrison and Lady Henley were in the morning room playing backgammon and looked up in surprise as he was announced. "Kitty!" gasped Mrs. Harrison. "Is she all right?"

The Baron drew a chair up to the backgammon table and sat down. "That is what I mean to find out. Does your daughter think that she is in love with me, ma'am, and does she also think that I am in love with her?"

"But — of course," Mrs. Harrison faltered. "Don't you remember our agreement?"

Peter took a deep breath. "I am asking you if Kitty has any idea that I have been bought?"

Mrs. Harrison flushed an ugly color and for once was speechless.

Lady Henley slowly masticated a macaroon. "She didn't know the first thing about it, Peter. I thought with all your experience with women you would know how to handle a gentle filly like that."

Peter Chesworth regarded both women with horror. The enormity of his behavior rushed into his mind and he nearly writhed with misery.

"How could you do that to the girl?" he

said icily. "You are nothing better than a couple of Covent Garden madames."

Mrs. Harrison hung her head, but Lady Henley eyed him coldly. "There's a pretty nasty name applies to you. You ain't nothing but a sort of gigolo yourself."

Lord Peter Chesworth got to his feet and looked at Lady Henley with icy hauteur. "How dare you. I . . ." Then a slow grin crossed his face. "Lady Henley, you have just put a backgammon counter into your mouth."

Lady Henley looked unconcerned. "Wondered why these macaroons were so hard." She calmly took it from her mouth, placed it on the board, and lifted the macaroon she had been mistakenly using as a counter and popped it in her mouth.

"Sit down again, Peter," she said. "We've all been carried away and have made a mess of things. What are we going to do?"

Lord Chesworth sighed heavily. "At the moment, all I suggest is that I take her to Reamington Hall today as planned and begin to treat her like the innocent young girl she is."

"That's it," said Lady Henley. "Give her a bit of fun too. I don't think she's had much so far."

Mrs. Harrison blushed guiltily. "There,

there, Euphemia," said Lady Henley with surprising kindness. "You can't go on blaming yourself. We'll just need to sort things out the way we can."

Mrs. Harrison was the first person to arouse anything approaching warmth in Lady Henley's fatty heart. Mrs. Harrison had fed her well, deferred to her and paid her debts. No one had ever done as much before. A strong bond of loyalty and friendship had sprung up between the unlikely pair.

With a heavy heart, Peter Chesworth returned to his new town house and entered his wife's bedroom on tiptoe, feeling like a criminal.

She lay with her long dark hair fanned out on the pillow. Her cheeks were smudged with tears and she slept heavily like a tired child. He was just about to leave when she opened her eyes wide and stared at him like a cornered animal.

He sat down on the edge of the bed and took her hand in his. "Kitty. I owe you an apology for last night. I was very drunk and did not mean a word I said. Can you forgive me?"

Kitty looked at him doubtfully, in silence.

He went on. "We'll go to Reamington today. You'll like that, won't you? We'll pay calls on all the neighbors and — and — you can have a pony of your own."

Kitty brightened with excitement. "I would love that, my Lor— I mean, Peter."

"That's my girl." He leaned forward and gave her a brotherly kiss on the cheek, trying not to notice when she flinched.

"Now get dressed, my dear. I'll wait for you downstairs."

After he had left, Kitty flew around the room looking for her prettiest dress. The world had miraculously righted itself. She was about to pack her trunks when she remembered that that was the duty of her maid. Perhaps she might even begin to like Colette.

When they were seated in the railway carriage, the Baron handed Kitty a parcel. "I bought you something to read on the train," he said and, as she unwrapped it, he went on. "It's a book about all the sorts of birds and animals you'll find around Reamington."

"Oh, thank you, Peter," said Kitty, her eyes like stars.

He gave her another parcel. Bubbling with excitement she opened it. It was a box of chocolates with a picture of two children standing in front of a thatched cottage on the front. He was mocking her after all. She had not forgotten the gibe about chocolate-box art. But Peter Chesworth *had* forgotten and wondered what on earth was up with the girl now.

Kitty's first sight of Reamington Hall in all the glory of a lazy June afternoon, took her breath away.

It was a gem of a Georgian mansion, gleaming against its background of huge old trees and rolling lawns. The brougham came to a stop before the severe classical grandeur of the entrance and Kitty was led into her country home. As in town, the staff were gathered to meet her, from the butler down to the housemaids. But there was a difference. The friendly country faces smiled. Everyone seemed delighted to see her.

And when she went up to her rooms on the second floor and found vases of wild flowers arranged around the room, and the chintz curtains billowing in the summer breeze from the open windows, she felt almost at home.

She quickly donned her new riding dress, rejoicing in the brief absence of Colette who was following with the luggage and the Baron's valet. She took off her heavy stays and threw them on the bed. She would go unencumbered for once. Her gray gabardine riding dress with the velvet insets on the collar and her smart bowler made her feel like a new person.

Her husband obviously thought so as well. "That outfit becomes you. We must begin your riding lessons right away," he said. He was wearing jodhpurs and an old hacking jacket with patches on the elbows, and Kitty reflected that he even managed to make that comfortable outfit look elegant.

Well pleased with each other, they went out into the blazing sunshine and headed for the stables. "I am starting your training on a pony," said Lord Chesworth. "We'll get you onto something more ambitious later. What do you think of him? His name's Carrots."

A beautiful little piebald pony had been led out for her inspection. Kitty patted his glossy mane and prayed that this fairy tale would not fade.

As she was stammering out her thanks, a footman came running from the house. "Mr. Bryson wants to see you. He says it is very urgent, my Lord. He is waiting for you in the estate office."

His lordship groaned. "Bryson is the estate manager. If he says it is urgent then it must be." He called over one of the grooms. "Hanson, teach my wife to ride, will you? Just a few beginner lessons. Kitty, do forgive me." He gave her his charming smile and strode off in the direction of the house.

Kitty felt a pang of disappointment. But Carrots was nuzzling in her pocket, searching for sugar, so she turned to the groom and prepared to master the art of riding.

When Kitty at last returned to her rooms to change for dinner, she was feeling happy and exhilarated. Hanson had said she would make a good horsewoman. But her happiness died when she realized her husband did not intend to join her. He emerged briefly from the estate office to explain. "Things are in a terrible muddle, Kitty. I'm afraid that because of —" he was about to say "lack of money" but decided it would not be tactful "— because of my neglect, there is a lot to be done on the estate."

He ran his long fingers through his black curls. "I had hoped to have time to take you around. I tell you what I'll do. Our neighbors, the Thackerays, are giving a house party. I'll escort you there tomorrow and there I must leave you for a few days."

"But I would much rather stay here with you and my pony," said Kitty, almost in tears.

The Baron was irritated. He hoped, callously, that she was not going to turn into one of those clinging vines.

"Come now, Kitty. You need some fun to cheer you up. There are a lot of young people staying with the Thackerays." He tried to joke. "You should leave an old fogey like me to get on with my work."

"You're not old. You're only thirty!" said Kitty, the tears beginning to stand out in her eyes.

What a watering pot, thought the exasperated Baron. He must decide what was best for her.

"Don't be silly," he said, unconsciously imitating her mother. "You'll like it when you get there." With that, he escaped from the room.

Kitty sat miserably by herself through the nine courses of dinner, too downhearted to tell the butler that she was not hungry.

Afterward, she lay awake, reading in her room, waiting for the sound of her husband's footsteps on the stairs. At last, she could hear him. Dressed in her filmy nightdress with her fine, silky hair brushed on her shoulders, she sat up and listened. The footsteps hesitated for a second outside her door and then went on down the corridor. For a long time, she sat there, staring at the door, feeling like a foreigner adrift on some strange and alien sea.

The Honorable Mr. and Mrs. Jeremy Thackeray were waiting for them when they arrived the next day. As they stood on the steps of their home, both husband and wife seemed to be completely round, like Tweedledum and Tweedledee.

Called Rooks Neuk, the Thackeray home was modern, complete with electricity and steam heat which required the services of three resident engineers and two firemen, to maintain. It was built on the lines of a medieval castle including battlements and a fake armory. Various statues of heraldic beasts sported on the lawns and, to complete the picture, a sturdy drawbridge spanned a weedy moat.

The honeymoon couple were welcomed enthusiastically by the Thackerays. Mrs. Mary Thackeray may have been a round dumpling of a woman, but she was very smartly dressed. Kitty was glad that she had worn her new tea gown.

Mrs. Thackeray took her arm and surveyed her. "Love your teagie. Fittums! Fittums! Was it ex-pie?"

Kitty looked at her in surprise and turned to her husband for help, but he was deeply involved in conversation with the Honorable Jeremy. She took a deep breath and decided she must learn to cope with awkward social situations herself. After all, Miss Bates had always told her pupils, "When speaking to a foreigner, who has not a complete command of our splendid language, always speak very loudly and clearly."

"*I'm afraid I do not understand you.* Please . . . repeat . . . what . . . you . . . have . . . just . . . said . . . very . . . slowly . . . and . . . clearly." Mrs. Thackeray took a step back. Kitty had shouted full in her face.

"I'm not deaf," she said crossly. "I said — oh, never mind, I'll show you your room." Kitty was very bewildered. Mrs. Thackeray spoke English after all. What had she meant? Her hostess stopped outside a door with Kitty's name written on it on a neat white card. "I hope you will be comfortable," said Mary Thackeray, looking at Kitty nervously, in case she should start shouting again. "Your husband's room is over in the other wing."

Here was another mystery! Was it usual to keep husband and wife so far apart, especially on their honeymoon?

Had she heard Mrs. Thackeray downstairs, she would have understood. "Why didn't you put the lovebirds together?" asked Jeremy Thackeray.

His wife settled herself comfortably into an armchair like a roosting pigeon. "Well, first — he's not coming to stay until after two days, and second — have you forgotten that Mrs. Jackson's on the guest list?"

"Well, what's that to do with it? That's all finished, surely," answered her husband.

"Not a bit of it. Veronica Jackson told Harriet Croombe who told Betty Jamieson who told Alice Fairbrother who told me, that he spent his wedding night in her bed. Peter will want to be near his dear mistress. He only married that little gel for her money. Strange little thing. Kept shouting at me."

Lord Chesworth called in at his wife's room before he left. Kitty told him of Mrs. Thackeray's strange conversation.

"It's the new small talk," he explained. "She was merely complimenting you on your tea gown, saying it was an excellent fit and asking you if it were expensive. I heard you shouting at her."

"I thought she was a foreigner," said poor Kitty.

Peter Chesworth groaned. "Oh, well, she'll probably think you were playing a joke on her. The Thackerays and their friends love practical jokes. Which reminds me — have you examined your bed?"

Kitty shook her head. He crossed over and ripped back the covers. Kitty screamed as two small hedgehogs made a bid for freedom. "Poor little things," said the Baron, "they could have suffocated. I'll take them outside. Give me that hatbox over there. Don't look so dismayed, Kitty. It's only meant as a friendly joke."

But after he had left, Kitty looked dismally at the bed, imagining what it would have been like to have thrust her feet down at night under the covers. The poor things would have been dead by then. She did not think it was funny. She thought it was senseless and cruel.

She was called at five-thirty. Charades were to be performed in the music room. Kitty felt better. She loved amateur theatricals, but hoped that she would not be asked to perform.

When she arrived at the music room, the curtains had already been drawn to create theatrical darkness. There was no time to meet the other guests. She was shown to a chair facing a small stage which had been erected at the end of the room. Shuffling and excited giggles came, from time to time, from behind the stage curtains which were finally drawn to reveal Percy Barlow-Smellie. "Our charade tonight," he announced, "is called 'The Taming of the Shrimp' and you all must guess *who*."

The curtains closed for a minute and then swung back to reveal a young man dressed as Mercutio. His tanned face had been whitened and he wore a mop of glossy black curls. Opposite him, Kate was played by Veronica Jackson who wore a drab dress and a brown wig. "Come, kiss me, Kate," roared Mercutio. "Oh, reelly, I don't know as I should. Is it a refeened thing to do?" simpered Kate. The audience roared with laughter as the sketch went on in the same manner. One after another they began to call, "Got it! It's the Baron and the shopgirl."

All Kitty's little bit of happiness generated by her splendid country home and her new pony faded away and she sat mute, looking down at her hands like a hurt child. At last the dreadful charade came to an end and the lights went up.

There were horrified murmurs when the lights went on to reveal Kitty sitting there. She heard someone say, "It's really too bad of Veronica. I didn't know Lady Chesworth was going to be here." But Veronica did, thought Kitty, as the blue eyes stared across at her with a kind of lazy insolence. Even Mrs. Thackeray felt things had gone a bit too far, and was relieved when dinner was announced.

Dinner was a twenty-course nightmare, studded with vulgar practical jokes. Entrées heaved as if on a stormy sea because the hostess had put inflatable bladders under the plates, bon-bons flew up in the faces of the guests with a whirring noise as their clockwork mechanisms were released by the unwrapping of the silver paper, and one young matron was the *succès fou* of the evening by having a bustle which played "God Save the King" every time she sat down.

Kitty hoped to escape when dinner was over, but there was bridge and baccarat to be played until two in the morning and then another interminable wait while the whiskey-and-sodas and chicken sandwiches were brought in.

All the time Kitty prayed for the courage to leave. But the thought of getting to her feet and making her good-nights in front of this bright, malicious crowd terrified her.

At last she reached the safety of her bedchamber and with her heart in her mouth, ripped back the bedclothes.

The bed was thankfully empty of small creatures and booby traps. It looked comfortable and the sheets smelled of lavender. Kitty tore off her clothes and plunged between the covers like a small, frightened animal burrowing into its lair.

For two hours, she lay listening to scuffling and whispering from the corridor. What on earth was going on? Perhaps they were planning some jolly jape like setting fire to her rooms. At last the rustling died away and she fell asleep, longing for the strength and company of her elegant husband.

The morning dawned dark and depressing with sheets of rain thudding down on the lawn and filling up the weedy moat.

Kitty climbed into her clothes without the courage to ring for her maid. She met Mrs. Thackeray who was crossing the hall. "You are a bit early, my dear," she said.

"It's only ten-thirty. But you'll find we have a new guest in the breakfast room. The Bishop of Zanzibar. Charming man." And with that she hurried off.

Relieved to find that an important member of the clergy was part of this naughty world, Kitty opened the door. The Bishop, a surprisingly young, dusky-complexioned man, was already eating his breakfast. Kitty murmured a shy good-morning and moved to the sideboard. What a bewildering array of dishes! Where did one begin? There was enough to keep the Camden Town Pugsleys in food for a year.

There were about thirty different dishes including porridge, cream, coffee, cold drinks, Indian and Chinese tea, bacon, ham, sausages, poached and scrambled eggs, deviled kidneys, haddock, tongue, pressed beef and ham, fruit, scones, toast, marmalade, honey, and jam.

Kitty took a little scrambled egg, some toast and tea and sat down opposite the Bishop. Here was the help she needed to guide her in this bewildering social world. Kitty had been brought up Anglican to the backbone.

She heard movements upstairs and realized that the rest of the guests would soon

91

be joining them. "My lord Bishop . . ." she began tentatively.

"Yes, my child," he inquired. He seemed to have very kind, merry eyes.

"I am in need of advice and help," said Kitty. "Perhaps — if you could spare me some of your time. I would like to talk to you in private."

The Bishop surveyed her. "By all means, my dear. Shall we say in the library at noon? Good, good."

The rest of the guests began to arrive so Kitty made her escape, feeling as if a little of the burden had been lifted from her heart.

As the clock in the hall struck twelve, she pushed open the door of the library and blinked at the darkness. The curtains had been drawn but she noticed the Bishop sitting by the light of one lamp burning on a table next to the fireplace.

"Come forward, my child," he said, stretching out a gloved hand in welcome.

Kitty sat down primly on a chair facing him.

"Why don't you begin at the beginning, my child?" he said in a kindly voice. "Things are sometimes easier that way."

So, in a faltering voice, Kitty began to

tell him her story from the beginning, her voice gradually becoming stronger and more confident under his sympathetic attention.

She began to falter again as she described the horror of her wedding night. "My lord Bishop, I had never seen — a — a naked man before. And then he laughed at my picture."

"What picture, my child?" asked the Bishop in a muffled voice. Kitty tried to read his expression but his hand was in front of his face and his head was bowed.

"Oh, it's a darling picture. I bought it myself in Hampstead in this little shop next to Carson's bakery. There are these two children running across a meadow with their dog and there's a dear little thatched cottage in the distance and —"

Kitty stopped in surprise. Tears were running down the Bishop's dusky cheeks. He was moved by her story!

Then in the glow from the lamp, she noticed that each salt tear was cutting a clean white line down his face, and he was laughing. Oh, God! He was laughing as if he would never stop. The harsh mocking sound reverberated around the room. There were more sounds of laughter. Then a roar of "Surprise!" as the lights were switched on and the rest of the guests burst out from behind screens in the corners of the room.

"Oh, Cyril, you were magnificent," they screamed to "the Bishop" who was still laughing and mopping the dark stain from his face with his handkerchief.

It had all been another terrible practical joke.

"What on earth is going on?" demanded an imperious voice from the doorway. One of the most elegant women Kitty had ever seen stood surveying the room with cold contempt. Pastel-colored tulle that could only have come from Paris, swirled about her body in elegant lines. Her hat balanced on top of her golden curls was a frothy confection of the same tulle. She had small eyes and a large patrician nose which seemed to emphasize her general air of *chic* rather than detract from it.

Without waiting for a reply to her question, she walked straight up to Kitty and held out her hand encased in a pink kid glove. "I've come especially to meet you, Lady Chesworth," she said in a light, pleasant voice. "May I introduce myself since no one else seems able to? I'm Emily Mainwaring."

Kitty had heard of Lady Mainwaring

through the medium of the gossip columns. King Edward himself had called her the smartest woman in London.

"I have called to invite you to take a drive with me," she went on.

Kitty nodded her assent. She would have gone for a drive with Lucifer himself in order to get out of that dreadful room and away from Veronica Jackson's mocking stare.

Outside, the summer sun was once again shining merrily.

Once in her open carriage, Lady Mainwaring tied a carriage veil over her hat and called to the coachman to "spring 'em."

Kitty thought that nothing else could surprise her that horrid day. But she was wrong. As the carriage bowled past the lodge gates at a fast clip, Lady Mainwaring said, "I'm kidnaping you, you know."

Kitty gasped and clutched at the side of the swaying vehicle. Lady Mainwaring laughed. "I've got the best intentions," she shouted above the noise of the rushing wind made by the speed of the carriage. "We're stopping for lunch at the nearest inn and I'll tell you all about it."

Kitty sat in silence watching the summer scenery flashing past. The hot sun was drying up the puddles in the road and sparkling raindrops hung from the wild roses on the hedgerows. She decided she didn't care if she were being kidnaped. She never wanted to return to Rooks Neuk again.

The horses slowed to a canter, then a trot, and turned into the pleasant courtyard of an old coaching inn.

"We didn't need to go as fast as that," explained Emily Mainwaring blithely. "I just like a touch of the dramatic now and then. Very good for restoring the spirits."

Kitty's spirits began to soar. She had a sudden feeling that all her nightmares were coming to an end. She followed her companion through the public rooms of the inn and out into a sunny garden at the back.

Lady Mainwaring waited until the landlord's wife had finished drying the rain-spattered table and then unfurled her parasol and leaned back in her chair.

"I called to visit my old friend Amelia Henley," she said. "I'm sorry I missed your wedding but I happen to have just got back from Rome.

"Well — Lady Henley — after she had finished eating a whole goose, bones and all, I assure you — told me that she and your mother had made a cruel mess of your marriage arrangements and she begged me to help.

"The whole thing intrigued me so I drove down to Reamington Hall to find your husband up to his neck in the estate books. Where was his wife? I asked. He replied that you were having a high old time with the Thackerays. Now no one — unless they have the hide of a rhinoceros — has a high old time at the Thackerays. So I didn't say anything to him. I just rode to the rescue.

"Now, tell me all about it."

Lady Emily's honesty was patent and so for the second time that day, Kitty told her story.

"Just what I thought," said Lady Mainwaring when she had finished. "Look, Kitty — I may call you Kitty, may I? — I will send my coachman back to Rooks Neuk — dear God, *what* a name — to collect your baggage. You shall come back to London with me and by the time I've finished with you, you will be the smartest matron in town and all the young men will be at your feet."

"I don't want all the young men at my feet. Only my husband," cried Kitty.

"You are not going to get your husband

97

at your feet the way you are now," said Lady Mainwaring briskly. "You have allowed yourself to be bullied unmercifully by all concerned. Now I am going to bully you, but only to put some stiffening into your backbone."

She looked at Kitty's pretty organza dress. "Who chooses your clothes for you?"

"My mama and Lady Henley," said Kitty.

"Choose your own always," said her new friend. "Clothes that someone else has imposed on you always sit on your body as if they don't belong to you. We will go to the dressmakers in London and you will choose exactly what you want to wear. It is no use wearing something in perfect taste if you don't *feel* pretty in it."

Lady Mainwaring twirled her parasol and looked on her new friend with amused kindness.

"The secret of social success is to do and say exactly what you want — within limits. If anyone is teasing you or being witty at your expense and you can't think of anything witty or clever to say in your defense — don't. Be damned rude. Be extremely honest always. Nothing frightens a social crowd more than honesty. And anyone they are frightened of — they make the current fashion.

"Care to give it a try?"

"Oh, yes," breathed Kitty. "But my husband. He is coming to meet me at the Thackerays tomorrow."

"You shall send him a loving little note," said Lady Mainwaring. "Say you are bored with the country and have gone with me to London for a short stay. Say you will miss him, but that you appreciate that he is too busy at the moment to have any time for you."

A shadow crossed Kitty's face. "You are in love with him, aren't you?" asked her companion. "Most women are. Your husband is a very attractive man who has been spoiled by too much feminine attention.

"You must make him run after *you*."

"Are you sure you are not mistaken?" asked Kitty timidly.

"Me?" said her ladyship forcefully.

"I, my dear, am *never* wrong."

Chapter Four

Lord Peter Chesworth closed the estate books with a weary sigh. An evening breeze brought in the heavy scent of lime from the old trees bordering the drive.

He had better set out in the morning to see how Kitty was getting along. After all, things were apt to get a bit rumbustious at the Thackerays'. He hoped they hadn't gone too far. His thin black brows met in a worried frown. Perhaps he should not have left her alone. He remembered the faint look of contempt on Lady Mainwaring's face when he had explained where Kitty was. With a pang, he suddenly remembered being seventeen himself when everything had seemed to matter so much, a gangling youth standing nervously at his first ball, frightened by the chattering sophistication of the older debutantes.

Well, he would rescue her tomorrow and perhaps take her to the seaside. He frowned again. Why had the word "rescue" entered his mind?

When he arrived at Rooks Neuk at noon

on the following day, the guests were just finishing breakfast. Veronica Jackson immediately came fluttering up to him, but of his wife there was no sign.

Mrs. Thackeray handed him a note.

His thin face flushed angrily as he read Kitty's letter. She had no right to go off without waiting to see him. Then let her have her independence. He would continue to put his affairs in order. He had no intention of rushing up to town. It would teach her a lesson.

He refused offers of breakfast, abruptly made his good-byes and, clutching Kitty's note in his hand, marched out to his carriage.

Veronica Jackson came fluttering after him. "Why can't you wait, Peter? It's not like you not to make the most of an opportunity."

Peter Chesworth studied the weed in the moat. "I have a lot of work to do, Veronica."

She pressed closer to him. "But your little shopgirl isn't waiting for you, is she?"

He turned and looked down at her, an unfathomable expression in his light eyes. "Don't call my wife by that silly name, Veronica. I must leave. Good-bye."

He strode off across the drawbridge,

leaving an angry Veronica to stare after him. She would have been even angrier, if she could have realized what he was thinking.

Lord Peter Chesworth was thinking of his wife. He was remembering her delicate figure, shy voice, and large gray eyes. By comparison, Veronica seemed . . . well . . . somehow overblown.

Kitty was at that moment sitting in the pretty garden of Lady Mainwaring's Regents Park home and wondering why her husband had not come after her.

At last, she voiced her thought aloud. Lady Mainwaring put down her gardening tools and turned to look at her.

The garden, which was Lady Mainwaring's pride and joy, sloped gently down to meet the Regents Park canal. It glowed with every kind of English garden flower — stocks, sweet william, pansies, marigolds, lupins, and delphiniums. Rambling roses rioted up the iron trelliswork on the white walls of the house and over by the garden wall, a bed of herbs added its heady scents to the summer air — thyme, marjoram, basil, parsley, and mint. A huge weeping willow trailed its long fingers in the green waters of the canal and its fluttering leaves sent dancing patches of shadow over Kitty's troubled face.

She was seated at a small cane table by the water's edge. In her pink-and-white spotted organza dress with the high, boned collar and her broad-brimmed picture hat, she looked as if she had stepped out of a French painting, reflected Lady Mainwaring. Monet — or was it Manet?

"Are you thinking about your husband again?" she teased Kitty. "Well, don't. He will have received your note and, with any luck, will be furious at you. Any reaction is better than none, my dear. In about two days' time, in my estimation, he will decide to come and see what we are up to, but you, of course, will not be here."

"Why not?" asked Kitty faintly. She had done nothing but look forward to her husband's arrival.

"Because you are not ready yet," said Lady Mainwaring, picking up a trowel and returning to work. "Your maid, Colette, for example, is boasting that she does no work. I *always* listen to servants' gossip. It may be vulgar but it is a very valuable source of information. How else would I have known that Lady Jessingham meant to cut me at the opera? She told her personal maid who told her sister who is walking out with one of my footmen who told *my* personal maid who told me. So *I* cut the old bat before she had a chance to cut me first.

"But what were we talking about? Ah, yes, Colette. We are going out to tea at the Barlowe-Smellies' — Percy's parents. Ring for your maid to help you change and dismiss her if she shows the slightest sign of insolence. That is your first dragon. Secondly, what do you think of Percy Barlowe-Smellie?"

Kitty thought back to her wedding and to the poems and antics of the best man. "I think he's a horrid young man," she said.

"Then you must tell him," said Lady Mainwaring. "But first you must deal with Colette."

Wishing heartily that she were once again Miss Kitty Harrison of Hampstead instead of the Baroness Reamington, Kitty trailed off slowly indoors.

When she reached her room, she sat looking at the old-fashioned bellpull as if it were some species of venomous snake. But Emily Mainwaring had said she would lose her husband if she continued to be timid. At last, she reached out and gave the bell-pull an enormous jerk. She waited ten minutes in fear and trepidation until the door opened.

"You rang, Ma'am?" Colette strolled into the room, the flicker of veiled insolence lurking in her black eyes.

"Please help me dress. I am taking tea with the Barlowe-Smellies," said Kitty in a firm, clear voice.

"What d' ye want to wear?" said Colette lazily, looking out of the window at the garden.

There was a long silence. She turned slowly from the window. Her mistress was looking at her with a distinctly imperious glare. Colette was not to know that in taking her time in turning around, she had given Kitty the necessary courage to conjure up that expression.

"If you don't know your job," said Kitty in a voice like brittle glass, "you may leave my service this instant."

Colette ducked her head to hide her surprise and bobbed a curtsy.

"I'll see to it right away, Ma'am."

Kitty's hard, light voice went on. "Must I keep telling you how to do your job? You will address me as 'my Lady' in the future — at all times. Do you understand?"

"Yes, ma— my Lady."

Kitty's small stock of courage ran out. But she kept her voice on the same hard tone. "Very well. You may leave. I will dress myself this once since I am very displeased with you."

Colette scuttled from the room with bowed head. The other servants had warned her that she was going too far. They had told her of the long, miserable queues of unemployed waiting outside the agencies and that a Baroness could have her pick of personal maids any day of the week.

After Colette had left, Kitty looked down at her trembling hands. She couldn't go on with this. She just couldn't!

She said as much to Lady Mainwaring as they prepared to leave for the tea party. "Don't worry," said her friend. "The first few battles are always the worst."

The carriage rolled through the streets in the direction of Kensington and Kitty could not help looking for a tall, familiar figure with curly black hair.

They were bowling along past the entrance to the zoo when Kitty spied two familiar figures and gave a sharp cry of recognition. Lady Mainwaring signaled the coachman to stop and the carriage backed up to the couple standing on the pavement. It was Hetty Carson with John Stokes. Hetty was wearing a smart plaid dress, her jaunty ringlets bobbing with excitement. John Stokes was wearing his Sunday best and obviously feeling the heat. His high, hard collar, which, like everything about him, was too tight, was cutting into the sides of his chubby face.

"Why Kitty! You look so grand!" screamed Hetty. Then she pouted. "Why didn't you invite me to your wedding?" Kitty stammered and blushed until Lady Mainwaring said, "I am afraid Kitty had nothing to do with the guest list. Her mother arranged everything."

"Oh, that explains it," said Hetty angrily. "Kitty's my best friend — aren't you, Kitty? — and I knew she would never forget me. When are you going to invite me to your new home?"

Kitty stammered, "Well — I — I'm not staying at home right now. I'm staying with my friend — oh, I forgot to introduce you." Lady Mainwaring bowed and smiled and then sat back, feeling that she had helped Kitty enough.

Kitty looked hopefully at her, hoping Lady Mainwaring would ask Hetty to call on them, but her ladyship was giving all her attention to a couple of buskers outside the zoo and Kitty could not catch her eye.

"I shall send you a card when I am at

home again," said Kitty. "And you too, John. You know I won't forget you, Hetty," she added warmly.

Hetty smiled and dimpled. "Oh, thank you," she gushed. "I always say, old friends are the best, don't you think so, Lady Mainwaring?"

"No," said Lady Mainwaring uncompromisingly.

Hefty flushed with annoyance. "Well, our Kitty knows what I mean. Mustn't keep you. Ta-ta, Kitty. See you soon."

John Stokes mumbled and raised his hand in salute as the carriage rolled off.

"Encroaching little thing," said Lady Mainwaring, unfurling her parasol.

Kitty flared up, surprising herself at her own burst of temper. "If becoming socially acceptable means becoming a snob, I would like to stop right now," she raged.

But Emily only smiled. "You'll see, my dear. Just wait and you'll see."

Percy's father was a retired Indian army colonel and his family home abounded in brass mementos of the East, from coffee tables to gongs. The colonel, a middle-aged man with terrifying mustaches and angry-looking broken veins, emerged briefly to welcome them and tell them that this tea business was a lot of rubbish, give him a good Scotch any day, what, but his wife would look after them.

Mrs. Barlowe-Smellie was a thin, anemic woman with wispy hair and a breathless voice. She ushered them out into the garden, chattering busily. "So kind of you to . . . so busy . . . Indian or Chinese . . . ? you must try these . . . delicious . . . I get them from . . . where *is* Percy . . . ? introduce Mrs. Betty Simpson . . . Mrs. Edith Haughton . . . Mrs. . . . oh, dear . . . and James Dubois . . . not French . . . Somerset Dubois . . . and Henry ah . . . oh dear . . . there!"

She sat down triumphantly at the tea table and started dispensing cups with the satisfied air of someone who had just coped with a difficult situation.

Her son Percy breezed in and his eyes alighted on Kitty with a look of gleeful malice. "Well, well, Baroness," he said, coming to sit beside her. "How's things in Hampstead?"

"I don't know," said Kitty. "I haven't been back there."

"Quite right," said Percy rudely. "Cut the old connections."

"I have no intention of cutting my old connections," said Kitty tremulously, thinking of Hetty.

"For heavens' sakes, drink your tea, Percy, and stop chattering," snapped Lady Mainwaring. But Percy was in full cry.

"I've always wondered what you lot get up to in those little houses on the Heath. Bags of middle-class sin behind the old lace curtains, what?" He grinned, winked at the company, and helped himself to cream and sugar.

It was now or never. Kitty said in a very loud voice, "I think you are an absolutely horrid young man!"

Percy blushed. Everyone stared. Percy's mother surprisingly flew to Kitty's rescue. "Quite right, my dear . . . tell him so myself . . . cheeky, very cheeky . . . pinches housemaids' bottoms . . . very hard to get good girls these days . . . bad, yes . . . good, no . . . cook got drunk . . . cooking sherry . . . but it's the principle of the thing I always say . . . ," she ended happily.

Everyone breathed a sigh of relief and burst out talking at once about the age-old problem of servants.

"Very good," said Lady Mainwaring in a whisper to Kitty. "Now carry on as if nothing had happened."

Percy, to Kitty's surprise, began to talk to her in almost deferential tones about a play he had seen the night before. The rest of the company cut into his conversation, from time to time, asking Kitty how she was enjoying her new home and asking when her husband would be returning to London.

Kitty forced herself to answer their questions at some length, instead of just saying "yes" and "no."

When she and Lady Mainwaring rose to take their departure, Mrs. Barlowe-Smellie asked if they could come to dinner the following week.

"I'm afraid not," said Lady Mainwaring, drawing on her long gloves. "We are both in the need of sea air. We shall probably be in Hadsea or somewhere."

Mrs. Barlowe-Smellie expressed her disappointment in her usual fragmented way. "So very, *very* sorry. . . . Seaside . . . ? dear me . . . must be . . . well, you know . . . time of year . . . mashers . . . common people . . . tut . . . common . . . tut . . . but healthy . . . ozone . . . sea-bathing . . . prawns. I do so love prawns," she added, looking quite startled to find a complete sentence emerging from her lips.

When they were seated in the carriage, Lady Mainwaring turned to her companion. "You just slew dragon number

two. Did you notice how polite Percy became? He won't trouble you again. Now,
wasn't it worth the effort?"

Kitty nodded, feeling a faint, warm glow
of satisfaction.

"The next step," said her companion, "is
to remove ourselves from London before
your husband arrives."

"Perhaps he will be glad," cried Kitty.
"Perhaps the marriage will suit him better
this way."

"Nonsense," replied Emily Mainwaring.
"You are newly married. People will keep
asking for his wife. His wife isn't there. His
pride will be hurt. Be patient!"

Kitty reflected that her new friend always seemed to be too sure of everything.
Now Hetty, *she* would understand the un-
certainty of it all.

"I would like to visit Hetty before we
leave," she ventured timidly. "You know,
the old friend I met this afternoon at the
zoo."

Lady Mainwaring looked at her in silence for a minute. Then she said slowly,
"Yes, by all means. We have no engage-
ments for tomorrow afternoon and I wish
to work in my garden. But why don't you
go? You can use the carriage."

Kitty looked surprised. She had ex-

112

pected an argument. She could hardly wait to tell Hetty all her news.

Hetty was as excited as Kitty. The next day when Lady Mainwaring's smart carriage stopped outside the Carson home in Gospel Oak, Hetty ran out to meet Kitty, dancing with excitement.

"Oh, Kitty! Such a smart carriage and a groom as well as a coachman," she shrilled.

Kitty looked at the impassive back of the coachman and whispered, "Can't we go into the house, Hetty? I've such a lot to tell you."

"Go into the house!" exclaimed Hetty. "When you've got this spanking carriage and all? We'll go for a drive. Wait till I get my hat." And she ran back into the house before Kitty could reply.

She soon bounced out again wearing a huge purple toque on her glossy hair. Hetty, who had a generous allowance from Mr. Carson, had bought the hat for just such an occasion as this, despite the protests from her more sensible mother that it was headgear only suitable for a dowager.

"Where would you like to go?" asked Kitty.

"There's a darling tearoom in Belsize Park," bubbled Hetty, "with simply

113

scrumptious pastries."

Although she was a baker's daughter, Hetty had a seemingly endless appetite for pastry.

Kitty nodded, anxious to please her friend, but she could not help feeling disappointed. Her beloved Heath looked beautiful in the summer sunshine and she had imagined walking arm in arm with Hetty, away from the crowds, sharing confidences.

Her heart sank when they arrived at the tearoom. It was crowded with people, but the determined Hetty managed to find a table in the center of the room.

"Here's that very spot, Baroness," she said in a loud voice.

"What are you calling me 'Baroness' for?" whispered Kitty. Everyone was staring at them.

"You must try the pastries here, Baroness," roared Hetty, enjoying the sensation. " 'Member when we was — were — at school together, how we used to eat them?"

"Really, Hetty! Keep your voice down and *stop* calling me 'Baroness,' " said poor Kitty, her face flushing under the curious gaze of the rest of the people in the tearoom.

Hetty pouted. "You're no fun, Kitty. After all, you are a real-live Baroness and what's the point of being it if nobody knows?"

Unabashed, Hetty went on for the next terrible hour in the same way. It was "Baroness" this and "Baroness" that until Kitty felt ready to die with mortification. The only small grain of comfort to be had was that Hetty had assumed what she fondly believed to be an Oxford accent so no one could understand what she was saying. "Look at that dahling child with the fah hah, Baroness," she screamed, pointing to a blonde-haired infant at the next table.

Kitty could bear it no longer. "I must leave now, Hetty. I've got to get ready for the opera this evening."

Hefty's wide eyes gleamed. "Are you going with your husband, Baron Reamington?" she shrieked.

"No," whispered Kitty, hoping by the very softness of her voice to bring down the strident tone of Hetty's. "That's what I want to talk to —"

"You're probably going with one of your friends. A duke or an earl, I dessay."

Kitty paid for the tea and almost shoved her friend out of the tearoom and into the carriage. Hetty's forehead was glistening with sweat under the heavy velvet toque. "There," she said in more her normal voice, settling back in the carriage with a sigh of satisfaction. "That'll give all those snobbish old cats in Hampstead something to talk about. Hetty Carson having tea with a real-live Baroness!"

But by the time they reached her home in Gospel Oak, Hetty began to feel nervous. Perhaps she *had* overdone things a bit. She hugged Kitty. "I'm sorry, Kitty. I got so excited at seeing you again, I didn't give you a chance to talk. Please remember, your old friend Hetty is always here if ever you need help."

Kitty's heart was touched. She hugged her friend back and forgave her everything. "I'll come to call as soon as I get back, I promise," said Kitty.

Hetty climbed down from the carriage with a quick look up and down the street to see which of the neighbors was watching. She opened her mouth to point out that she could call at Kitty's new home, but shrewdly decided that her friend had had enough for one afternoon.

Kitty was very thoughtful on the road home but still loyal to Hetty. She had been awful in the tearoom but Hetty was a warm-hearted girl, she decided, and worth twice as much as any of her new-found society friends.

But Kitty still had to admit to herself that she was very disappointed. She had a longing to catch and reorganize some of her old life before she left for the sea. A woman trudged along the pavement, followed by a retinue of grubby children that marked out the burden of her yearly pregnancies. Kitty suddenly thought of the Pugsleys in Camden Town. Now that she was rich, she could surely do something better for them than serve out soup.

Feeling quite cheerful, she outlined her plan to Lady Mainwaring. Her ladyship looked at her young friend in some dismay. "It's very nice to play Father Christmas, Kitty, but don't get carried away. Start off helping them in a very small way and see how they can cope with it."

Kitty went off happily to make her plans and Lady Mainwaring stared at the photograph of her late husband in despair. Sir James Mainwaring had been a great philanthropist — in the drawing room. He wrote pamphlets and held forth, at length, on great schemes to help "the great unwashed." One militant lady had actually suggested, one day, that he should actually go out and do something about it. Sir

James had stalked off to his study in a sulk and the offending lady was never invited again. But the barb had rankled. Sir James had at last gone on an organized tour of the East End slums. It had caused a lot of publicity.

A photographer from the *Daily Mail* had asked him to pose holding a very dirty baby. Within two days, Sir James had contracted diphtheria and died.

Lady Mainwaring hoped Kitty knew what she was doing. Then she shrugged. There were some things that Kitty would just have to find out for herself.

Kitty had decided what to do. She remembered the Pugsleys' worn, chipped, and battered furniture. She would buy, and have delivered, new furniture to the house in Camden Town. With an energy and resolution that surprised her, she descended on Harridges in Knightsbridge and ordered a quantity of sturdy oak furniture and bedding to be delivered that day. The next day she received a letter by the first post.

"Dere, Miss," she read. "Thanking you for the furniteerr. We ar having a party on Satterday in your honor at nine in the eevning. Pleese to cum. Yrs. Freda Pugsley."

Lady Mainwaring tried to stop Kitty from attending, but Kitty would not change her mind. She longed to see all that sparkling furniture lighting up the Pugsleys' dingy home.

On Saturday morning she called on her mother and Lady Henley to tell them of her plans. Lady Henley was outraged. Exploding in a cloud of wine-biscuit crumbs, she told Kitty that the whole scheme was madness. Mrs. Harrison, however, seemed indifferent. "Go if you want," she shrugged, "but I would like a word with you in private before you leave."

Kitty followed her into the study. Mrs. Harrison's hair-pins seemed particularly agitated and popped out of her head like tiny bullets.

"Now, Kitty," said Mrs. Harrison, fixing her with a steely glare. "Has your marriage been consummated?"

Kitty blushed and shook her head.

"Good," said her mother unexpectedly. "I have prayed night and day for forgiveness. When I think of my pure daughter in the arms of that lecher . . ."

"But, Mama, he has only been a little wild in his youth like most young men," protested Kitty.

"You don't know what you're talking about," spluttered Mrs. Harrison. "Men! Dirty, filthy beasts. And that includes your father. His great hairy hands and his wet mouth and . . ." Mrs. Harrison put a trembling hand to her mouth to stop her own tirade.

Kitty got to her feet. "I admit my marriage has not begun well, Mama. But I love my husband and — and I know I can make him love me."

She waited a minute in silence but her mother's glittering eyes were fixed on the middle distance and her thin mouth was working with emotion. Kitty backed out of the door and went in search of Lady Henley.

Her ladyship was playing patience with one hand and eating asparagus with the other. A small river of butter dripped unheeded onto the cards.

Kitty sat down and watched, fascinated, as a new tributary of butter made its way down Lady Henley's neck and then joined up with another little river to form a mainstream that plunged into the cleavage and, she supposed, down into the stays. Kitty remembered the March Hare — "It was the *best* butter" — and started to giggle.

Lady Henley eyed her with disfavor.

"You're getting as dotty as your mother," she remarked.

"That's what I wanted to talk to you about," said Kitty. "Mama seems a little — well — strange."

"She'll get over it — I hope," said Lady Henley. "She's been torturing herself with remorse ever since your wedding."

"But I love my husband," said Kitty.

"Let's hope she realizes that," said Lady Henley. "But at the moment, she's going about wringing her hands and talking about lily-white maidens in the paws of lecherous beasts. Got the doctor to look at her, you know. He says she'll be all right with a bit of rest and quiet."

Kitty smiled with relief and went home to prepare for her expedition to Camden Town. Lady Mainwaring had insisted that a bodyguard of two footmen accompany her in the carriage. But when they arrived at the Pugsleys', Kitty begged the footmen to remain in the carriage. "I'm sure the Pugsleys would be embarrassed," she said. The coachman turned around. "Well, your Ladyship, I've got to keep my horses moving. I don't want them standing around too long."

"Call back for me in an hour," said Kitty. Really, the servants were worse than their

121

masters! What harm could come to her at the Pugsleys'? She had known them all her life.

Apart from having ten children, the Pugsleys also took in boarders and the three-story house seemed to be jammed with noisy people. Smelling strongly of gin, Mrs. Freda Pugsley ushered Kitty into the parlor. The friends, relatives, and family gave her three hearty cheers and Kitty blushed with pleasure. She accepted a glass of sherry and sat down and realized that the furniture was the same.

The armchair she was sitting in still reeked of cat and old baby vomit. The sofa was still spilling its innards on the floor and one leg of the table was still propped up with a copy of the Bible.

Everyone, including the Pugsley children, seemed to have been drinking a lot. Their faces were flushed, their voices raucous, flickering in the candlelight of the tenement, like a scene from Hogarth. The father, Mr. Bob Pugsley, who had been unemployed as long as Mrs. Pugsley could remember, was wearing the jacket of his soup-stained suit open to display a new waistcoat. Then he hitched up his trousers to display his new suspenders. "Let's see yer drawers, Bob," yelled one of the women and everyone screamed with laughter.

Kitty blushed and began to pray for the arrival of her carriage. But what had happened to the furniture?

Bob Pugsley was calling for music. A female of uncertain years who seemed to be some sort of aunt to the young Pugsleys, took up her stance beside the piano, and, to the accompaniment of much tinny battering of the keys by another female relative, began to sing a music-hall song.

The song dealt with the problems of a young miss who had lost her way on the railway system and was appealing to a porter for help, explaining that she had "never 'ad 'er ticket punched before."

What there was about this to cause such gales of salacious laughter was beyond poor Kitty.

She noticed one of the quieter boarders standing next to her and, under cover of the noise, asked him what had happened to all the new furniture.

"They sold it, your La'ship," he said.

"But why?" asked poor Kitty.

"Because money for the drink and the dogs means more to this lot than new furniture," he replied.

It couldn't be true! Kitty was nearly in

tears. "But I've visited them almost every Sunday since I was a child and I have never seen them with any drink."

The boarder looked at her as if she were a Hottentot. "Course you didn't! They does their drinking on Saturday. Never on Sundays. Very religious, is Mrs. Pugsley."

Kitty glanced at the watch on her bosom. Half an hour to wait. Please God, let something happen to get me out of here, she prayed.

Suddenly, through the noise and haze of cigar smoke and the capering figures, Kitty saw the dirty net curtains going up in an instant blaze.

Everyone began to scream at once and fight to get out of the door. But the parlor door was locked. Bob Pugsley was trying to push them back so that he could get space to charge the door but no one was listening. A woman's hair caught on fire and she screamed in agony. Flames were dancing around the room and setting the swinging skirts of the terrified women alight.

Kitty began to feel herself falling as the guests swayed backward and forward. Her skirt caught fire and she beat at it with her fingers. The press closed around her again and the room crackled and danced and swayed before her terrified eyes. Then there was a blessed rush of air from the door. Throwing themselves into the room, the footmen grabbed Kitty and unceremoniously dragged her out into the street where they rolled her on the ground and beat out the flames.

The clanging bell of the fire engine could be heard in the distance and soon the huge horses pulling it came charging down the street. Wrapped in rugs, Kitty sat in the carriage shivering with fright.

She became aware of a small, white, tear-stained face peering over the edge of the carriage door. It was the eleven-year-old Pugsley called Jane.

"Miss Kitty," she whispered. Kitty leaned over the open carriage. "Oh, miss," said Jane. "The fire. I saw a hand at the open window. It reached into the room and held a lucifer to the curtains," then Jane was swept away by her mother. Mrs. Pugsley was running from child to child, counting feverishly, losing the count, and beginning all over again.

"We can do nothing more here, my Lady," said the coachman. "Good thing we came back for you early. With your Ladyship's permission, I think we should go home."

And still shaking and huddled in her rugs, Kitty was borne off, back to the West End, where the passing throng stared at her smoke-streaked face in surprise.

Lady Mainwaring's excellent German butler informed Kitty that his mistress was at the theater and then proceeded to summon the staff: a footman to fetch the doctor, Colette to change Kitty's ruined clothes, the housekeeper to supply hot, sweet tea, bandages, and ointment.

The doctor fussed but said the burns were minor. He prescribed a sleeping draft and then left Kitty to her worried thoughts. She felt in some way that she had caused the disaster. Without the money from the furniture, the Pugsleys would not have gone in for such wild celebration. Jane's story of the hand at the window was simply the wild imaginings of a frightened child.

Mercifully, the sleeping draft began to take effect and Kitty, at last, closed her eyes.

Lady Mainwaring had, unfortunately, left instructions that the staff were not to wait up for her and had given her personal maid the evening off. It was not until the next day that she learned of the Pugsley fire. It had made headlines on the front page of *The Daily Mail,* including the sub-headline of the story which carried interviews with all the Pugsleys — "Baroness returns to scenes of childhood." Lady Mainwaring put down the paper and groaned aloud. What a lot of fun the gossips were going to have with that one. Best get Kitty out of town right away.

For once the calm and level-headed Lady Emily Mainwaring was shaken from her customary calm and in an effort to save Kitty from society's malicious gossips, she forgot all about the effect the news would have on Kitty's husband.

Lord Peter Chesworth was sitting, as usual, over the books in the estate office when he noticed the trim figure of Veronica Jackson on horseback, riding up the drive under the lime trees.

He had a sudden impulse to ring for the butler and say he was not at home. But as he sat undecided, the door behind him opened and the butler informed him that he had put Mrs. Jackson in the small salon. With a sigh, Peter Chesworth got to his feet.

As he entered the salon, Veronica swayed towards him and wrapped her arms around his neck. She pressed her lips to his and he felt all the old passion that she was able to arouse. But after a few minutes, he put her away from him. "You forget I'm now a married man."

Veronica was ruffled. "An unhappily married man," she said acidly.

"I do not wish to discuss my wife," said Lord Chesworth, in a flat voice.

Veronica became very angry. "Then you will not be interested in what your silly little shopgirl has been up to. Cavorting around Camden Town." She flung a copy of the *Daily Mail* down on the table and marched from the room.

Like many of his class, Peter Chesworth despised Lord Northcliffe's "cheap" newspapers and was heartily afraid of them. The reporters of the *Daily Mail* and its sister paper, the *Daily Sketch*, had a nasty habit of ferreting out a lot of accurate and unpleasant facts about their betters.

With a feeling of distaste, he picked up the paper and saw Kitty's name staring up at him from the front page. The reporter had done an excellent job. Everything in Kitty's young life was documented, from Miss Bates's seminary in Hampstead to her Sunday visits to the Pugsleys with her mother, and the fact that she was newly married and staying with Lady Mainwaring while her husband honeymooned alone in the country. He threw the paper away from him in disgust. What on earth was up with Lady Mainwaring? She had enough political influence to get a story like that stopped before it reached the presses.

Suddenly, the whole enormity of his marriage struck him. He had accepted the girl's money but that was all he had done. He had now made it clear to everyone that he did not care anything for Kitty. Well, she was his wife, his property. He would set off for London right away and bring her home.

Chapter Five

Kitty wriggled uncomfortably on the plush seat of the railway carriage. If she leaned her head back, the lace antimacassar caught in her hair. If she leaned forward, her stays jabbed her under the bosom. The carriage was stifling. Sweat trickled down Kitty's body and she desperately wished she could have a good scratch. She felt as comfortable as a dog with fleas.

"Emily, can't we *please* open the window?" asked Kitty.

"I'm afraid not," answered Lady Mainwaring. "Our dresses would be ruined by smoke and cinders. You will just have to suffer. Are you wearing stays?"

Kitty nodded and searched in her reticule for her book of *papier poudré*. The pads which she wore on her head *à la Princesse de Galles* to puff out her fine hair, the straw hat with its top-heavy pile of artificial fruit and flowers, and her long, tight, kid gloves worn above the elbow, made her feel as if she were encased in some extremely refined torture chamber.

"I think you should stop wearing stays, Kitty," said Emily. "It's not as if you need to."

"Leave off my stays?" gasped Kitty. She was as shocked as if Lady Mainwaring had suggested she leave off her knickers.

"Well, you're very slim and have a firm bust. Why suffer needlessly. Really, Kitty, no one would know."

Kitty was saved from replying as the train drew into Hadsea station. Both ladies stood for a moment as a cool sea breeze swept the scrubbed wooden platform. The train, which had made a special stop to set them down at the small resort, gave a great contemptuous cough and surged forward to the more fashionable resorts ahead.

They waited for the servants who had descended from a third-class carriage at the other end of the platform, to join them.

"I'll tell you a little bit more about our hosts as we go along," said Emily as they walked from the clean little station to where three carriages were waiting; one for the luggage, one for the servants, and one for themselves.

They drove down the little high street past the shops with their bunches of black sandshoes, shrimp nets, and revolving stands of colorful postcards, past the butcher's on the corner, where the jolly-looking butcher waved his straw hat to them in salute, then around the curve on the high street — and there was the sea!

Kitty let out a gasp of pleasure and clapped her hands like a child. The sea sparkled like blue sapphires all the way to the horizon. Little white sails of yachts in the distance sculled to and fro on the fresh breeze. The beach was a perfect curve of golden sand, edged with flat sandstone rocks studded with great clumps of sea pinks.

"Pay attention, Kitty," said Emily Mainwaring, smiling at her pleasure. "I'll tell you a bit about the people we are going to stay with. Mrs. Jane Dwight-Hammond is a poet. Not a very good one I'm afraid but she's a very kind lady. Her sister, Matilda, is also very nice but she has a penchant for collecting stray cats. I'm afraid the little brutes are all over the place. They are both maiden ladies and very old friends of mine."

"But you said *Mrs.* Dwight-Hammond," pointed out Kitty.

"Well, she was disappointed in love, or so she says, at a very early age and sees no reason why she should suffer the stigma of being a Miss. She invents husbands for herself but they're apt to change with the days of the week. Don't let it bother you. She's quite harmless. Also, it's good social training to get used to eccentrics. Goodness knows, society is peppered with them."

The house was called unimaginatively "Sea View" and stood on a small promontory at the far end of the beach. It was an enormous Victorian mansion with tall red roofs and it stood in several acres of neglected garden. As the carriages crunched to a halt on the graveled drive, no sound could be heard but the wind sighing through some ragged, monkey puzzle trees on the scraggly lawn.

"Ring the bell, Judson," said Lady Mainwaring to one of the footmen, "and keep on ringing. This always happens," she explained to Kitty. "They love company but they get very nervous when company actually arrives and go into hiding."

Judson rang the ship's bell which was on a stand outside the door. Then the silence fell again and faint, agitated rustling and scurrying could be heard from the back of the house. Just as Judson was about to sound off on the bell again, the front door popped open and a thin middle-aged lady in a shabby teagown rushed out. She had a thin, lined face and a great quantity of strong yellow teeth. Her pale, weak eyes watered in the sunlight and she peered at them anxiously.

"Oh, it *is* you, Emily. We can't be too careful you know. Lots of bad, bad men around."

This was Jane.

An identical figure came bounding down the steps behind her and hugged both Kitty and Lady Mainwaring in turn. "I forgot to tell you they were twins," said Emily Mainwaring to Kitty.

Matilda Dwight-Hammond did indeed look, at first glance, like a carbon copy of her sister. But closer inspection revealed her to be smarter in her dress and less vague and timid in her manner.

"Tea is served in the drawing room," said Matilda.

"Can we please change our gowns first?" asked Emily Mainwaring. "We're very sticky and hot from the train journey."

A look of almost childish disappointment crossed Matilda's face. "But Emily, teatime is *always* when we say 'hello.' "

"Oh, very well," sighed Emily. Matilda beamed with delight and ushered them into the drawing room. Kitty expected to find other visitors to whom she was expected to say "hello," but the eyes which met hers belonged to a score or so of cats.

There were cats sitting on the chairs, cats on the floor, even cats on the piano. Their different-colored furs gleamed with health and their unblinking eyes surveyed Kitty with interest.

"We'll start with the first," said Matilda, and then giggled. "Why, your name *is* Kitty. How suitable!"

She led the way to the first cat, a huge tabby with large green eyes. "Now this is Peter. Say hello to Kitty, Peter."

Peter mewed politely. They passed to the next. "And this is Tibbles." Tibbles was a Persian who fluffed her fur and also mewed.

More fascinated by the minute, Kitty was introduced to cat after cat. Then Matilda clapped her hands and opened the door. "Hellotime is over," she announced. "Time to leave." The cats rose and stretched and slowly loped from the room, quickening their pace as they went out into the garden, the sun shining on their sleek fur. Then they fanned out and dived off into the shrubbery.

"Now it's good-bye time," said Lady Mainwaring. "We really must get changed."

"Of course, of course," said Matilda. "I'll show you to your rooms."

Kitty stood patiently and let Colette undress her. Her room was charming. White lace curtains framed the long windows and were looped back to show a view of the beach and the sea on the other side of the tangled shrubbery of the garden.

The furniture was of white cane with the exception of a marble washstand with a porcelain ewer and basin which were overflowing with roses and maidenhair ferns. An empty crystal bowl stood next to the washstand on a triangular cane table. The sisters had forgotten to arrange the flowers or — more likely, thought Kitty — they considered the basin and ewer more suitable for a flower display.

Dressed in a loose, flowing teagown and minus stays, Kitty walked out onto a small wooden balcony in front of the window and took a deep breath. Far away, yachts skimmed across the horizon under a freshening breeze. Little puffs of clouds chased each other across the cerulean sky. On the shoreline, the shallow water changed from blue to pale-green and on a stretch of springy turf above the tide line, the cats romped and played, their fur rippling and glistening in the light wind.

Kitty could not help thinking it would have been the ideal place for a honeymoon. What on earth was her husband doing now?

Peter Chesworth was, at that moment, staring at Lady Mainwaring's butler as if he could not believe his ears.

"Gone to the seaside!" repeated his lordship angrily. "Did my wife leave a note?"

"No, my Lord," said the butler. "But Lady Mainwaring did."

Lord Chesworth removed his gloves, tucked his cane under his arm, and scanned the single sheet of paper. "Dear Peter," Lady Mainwaring had written, "Kitty was disappointed not to hear from you so we assumed you were still occupied with your work on the estate. We are going to Hadsea for a short holiday. May we hope that you will join us? I enclose the address. . . ."

He crumpled the note in his hand. No, they may *not* hope that he would join them. He had never had to chase after any woman in his life and he did not intend to start now — particularly with his wife who ought, by rights, to be sitting by his side warming his slippers and his bed.

He stood irresolute on the pavement and

then, with a slight feeling of being hunted, saw Veronica Jackson's carriage coming to a stop. The lady herself, to judge from the amount of luggage strapped on the back, had just returned from the country as well.

Peter Chesworth did not know that Veronica had watched him going into the house from the carriage window and subsequently seen him reemerge a few moments later with a look like thunder on his face.

"Well, Peter, here we both are back in town," she said brightly. "Are you running off anywhere?"

His lordship was absolutely furious with his wife. He was damned if he would go running after her.

"I'm going nowhere at present," he said, looking up at her with his attractive mocking smile. "But I'll take you to the opera this evening if you like."

"Not Wagner!" begged Veronica in mock horror. "I can't stand all that caterwauling."

"No, not Wagner," he assured her. "Bizet."

"Till tonight then!" She kissed her fingertips to him and her carriage moved off.

They arrived mercifully late and the production of *Carmen* was already halfway through the first act. Peter Chesworth was regretting his impulse. Perhaps if they stayed quietly in the box at the interval, they would not be noticed.

But as the lights blazed up at the first interval, Veronica was leaning over the edge of the box, waving to her friends. She seemed almost to be going out of her way to attract attention and was wearing a very low-cut dress which seemed to draw all the eyes of the men like a magnet.

With a shudder, Peter Chesworth saw his mother-in-law and Lady Henley in a box opposite. Lady Henley had her lorgnette positively screwed to her eyes and Mrs. Harrison was directing a pair of opera glasses in the direction of Veronica's white bosom.

Well, they could glare all they wanted. He was neither going to explain nor apologize. As Lady Henley made a movement to her feet, the theater was mercifully plunged into darkness as the second act began.

Lord Chesworth decided to escape. "Let's go to the Cavendish and drink champagne," and, as his partner showed signs of protesting, he clasped her hand. "Please, Veronica."

Veronica smiled in the darkness. They would by all means go to the Cavendish

Hotel and she would make sure that Peter Chesworth did not leave her till the morning.

Lord Chesworth guided his companion into the public dining room of the Cavendish in an effort to avoid the heavy-drinking crowd who gathered with the proprietress, Mrs. Lewis, in her parlor. But the dining room seemed to be filled to capacity with London society, Mrs. Lewis's reputation as a cook drawing them from all over.

Peter Chesworth's ears burned as glances were thrown in their direction and the feathered headdresses of the ladies bobbed and nodded as they whispered with their heads together. He wished for the first time in his life that he were a woman so that he could faint or, at the very least, complain of a headache. Veronica was drinking steadily and leaving much of the excellent food on her plate. Her eyes held a hectic glitter and her voice became louder and more strident until her personal endearments seemed to be bouncing off the walls. He suddenly thought of his quiet, shy wife and heartily wished he had gone to join her. He would leave for Hadsea in the morning.

But by the time he had got rid of a very angry Veronica on the doorstep of her home and reached the safety of his own bed, he decided to go in two days' time instead. He did not want to look as if he were running to heel like a whipped dog.

Kitty was enjoying the Dwight-Hammonds' eccentric household immensely. The sisters dithered about cheerfully, Matilda with her cats and Jane with her poems. Lady Mainwaring rested and read and chatted with the sisters, leaving her young friend endless freedom to explore the garden and the beach.

Playing with the cats, paddling at the edge of the water, collecting shells and seaweed, Kitty was like a child. She even inspired Jane Dwight-Hammond to write a poem in her honor. Jane gathered together Lady Mainwaring, her sister, Kitty, and the cats to listen to it.

Jane coughed nervously and fingered a long necklace of amber beads as she peered shortsightedly about the room to make sure she had her audience's full attention. She began:

"To Kitty.
  Running on the beach
  Seaweed in her hand
  Is she out of reach

Or just dancing on the sand
Does she wait a lover, I do ask
Or is she engaged in some other task . . . ?

A sudden clap of thunder shook the drawing room and the poetess threw her papers in the air and bolted out of the room.

Emily Mainwaring gave a very unladylike grin. "Jane is terrified of storms — thank goodness. I wonder how long that poem was going to be? 'The Lay of the Last Minstrel' is nothing compared to the length of some of Jane's epistles."

Matilda was as angry as that good-natured lady could be. "You are very, very cruel, Emily. Jane has a great talent. She would have been published by now if it weren't for *Them*." Kitty was to learn in due course that *"Them"* referred to the whole publishing world of men who, Jane and Matilda were firmly convinced, rejected the poems simply on the grounds that they were written by a woman.

A flash of lightning and another terrible roll of thunder rocked the house and died away leaving a dark, ominous silence, broken only by the faint whimpers of the terrified Jane abovestairs. "I had better go to her," said Matilda.

142

"What a frightful storm," said Emily. "We'd better go to sleep and have a rest before this evening."

The sisters and their guests had been invited to a ball at a country house five miles' distant. Their hostess, Maria Epworth, was an old schoolfriend of the Dwight-Hammonds.

Kitty lit the gas in her room and decided to read instead of going to bed, since the noise of the storm howling outside the shutters seemed to make sleep impossible. But for all the heavings and groans and shakes of the house as it rode out the storm, Kitty's eyes began to droop. She turned down the gaslight to a faint glimmer and climbed into bed, wriggling her toes down between the cool sheets. Her foot struck something thin and cold at the foot of the bed. It moved! Kitty screamed and leapt out of bed and stood with her bosom heaving. Then she laughed. Obviously the Dwight-Hammonds had gone in for the popular fad of practical jokes.

She ripped back the bedclothes and found herself staring down at the writhing bodies of two adders. Then she really screamed in earnest, stumbling through the old storm-rocked house, her terrified cries rising higher and higher over the noise of the thunder.

Lady Mainwaring was first on the scene to catch the frightened girl in her arms. "It must have been a nightmare, Kitty, but we'd better make sure."

The sisters did not keep any men-servants except for one very old deaf coachman. Neither the cook nor the housemaids would volunteer to go into Kitty's bedroom.

"In that case, I'll go myself," snapped Lady Mainwaring. With Kitty clutching her sleeve, she threw open the door of the bedroom. "There you are!" she exclaimed triumphantly. "Why there's noth—" Her voice broke off as she saw something moving on the floor and she edged into the room in time to see the tail of a snake disappearing as it slithered under the bed.

"Good God!" gasped Emily Mainwaring, leaning against the doorjamb.

"What is it?" cried Matilda, materializing behind them with her hair in curl papers.

"Snakes!" shouted Emily and Kitty together.

"Snakes! Are you sure?" screamed Matilda. And then without waiting for a reply, she threw back her head and yelled, "Cats. Cats! Come here, at once."

There was movement on the stairs and then the cats came bounding along the corridor. "Get the snakies. Get them!" shouted Matilda, dancing in excitement.

The women turned away and there was a great scuffling and mewing and then the leaders of the pack, who seemed to be Tibbles and Peter, strolled past them, each holding a dead snake triumphantly in its mouth. The other cats ambled past with a "see, there's nothing to it" attitude.

Clutching each other for support, the three women made their way downstairs and collapsed in the drawing room.

"My dear, dear Kitty. I am so sorry," gasped Matilda. "I've never known anything like it. There are adders up on the downs, of course. But in the house — and upstairs! Perhaps the storm drove them in." She rang for tea.

"Don't worry, my dear. My pussies shall patrol your room before you go into it at night."

A thin gleam of watery sunlight struck through the slats of the shutters. "There!" said Matilda triumphantly. "The storm is over. Open the shutters, Barker."

The housemaid threw open the long shutters and sweet, rain-washed air and sunlight flooded the room. Kitty felt her fears receding. Strange things happened in storms and things always did seem more frightening when the sky was black and the thunder rolled. And snakes were always said to make for the warmest part of a room.

Early that evening, as they were setting out for the ball, Kitty had almost forgotten about the incident except as a little adventure to tell her husband — if she should ever see him again.

As they climbed into the Dwight-Hammonds' elderly carriage, Barker came running out. "If you please, Mum," she addressed Matilda. "There's a person here what says you told him to make repairs to the roof."

Matilda flushed. Her memory was getting increasingly worse so she did not care to admit she had no recollection of ordering any such repairs. "Tell him to go ahead, Barker. But what an odd time of day to start work. I suppose the storm delayed him."

The carriage rolled off. Jane Dwight-Hammond was busily composing a poem about Kitty's adventure. "What rhymes with snake . . . hake . . . ? no, no . . . fake . . . perhaps . . . steak . . . oh, dear me, *no*."

By the time they reached the Epworths' home, she had successfully rhymed adder with badder, found it to be ungrammatical, and was nearly in tears from frustration.

Kitty entered into the lights and music of the Epworths' ball with a feeling of anticipation. Mr. and Mrs. Epworth were a kindly middle-aged couple and a good proportion of the young guests were pleasantly unsophisticated and pleased to have a pretty Baroness in their midst. Kitty's dance card was soon full and she twirled about the ballroom enjoying the novel feeling of success.

She was emerging from supper later in the evening on the arm of a young army captain who had been invalided home from the South African wars, when she looked across the ballroom and found herself staring at her husband. All thoughts of what had gone on between them on their wedding night, all Lady Mainwaring's advice, and all conventional behavior fled, as the Baroness Reamington flew across the ballroom and flung her arms around her husband's neck. Peter Chesworth hugged her slight body and stared down at his wife in surprise.

She looked incredibly pretty and fresh

with her wide gray eyes sparkling with delight and surprise. All his anger at her for having run away, all his fury at finding her gone when he arrived in Hadsea, fled before the warmth of her welcome. He drew her arm into his and led her out onto the terrace.

A small moon was racing between thin, high clouds as Peter Chesworth turned to his wife and said words she had longed to hear, "I've missed you, Kitty."

Slowly and confidingly, she put her arms around his neck. She saw the moonlight flashing on his pale eyes under their hooded lids and closed her own. She felt his lips against her mouth, pressing and exploring, his arms holding her closer. Kitty trembled in his arms as a tide of passion swept both of them. Finally, he raised his head.

"Let's go home before the others, Kitty," he whispered. "We have the whole night together in front of us."

Walking in a dream, Kitty said her goodbyes. The Dwight-Hammond sisters beamed on her fondly, Lady Mainwaring looked worried, as Kitty walked out to her husband's carriage. All the way back to the Victorian house, he held her hand and told her how much he loved her, really loved her, and Kitty felt almost drunk with so much happiness.

When they entered her bedroom, she turned and looked at him shyly. "I forgot to open the shutters and it's so stuffy in here . . ."

"Let me do it," said Peter Chesworth, moving past her.

"No," said Kitty. "I'll open them. It's my lovely view and I want to show it to you."

He sat down on the bed, smiling indulgently, as she threw open the shutters and stepped out onto the small balcony. She held out her hand. "Come and see. It's the most beautiful view in the world."

He moved slowly toward her. One minute she was standing there faintly lit by the moonlight, smiling at him and holding out her arms and the next, there was a hideous cracking sound and the balcony collapsed, hurling Kitty down into the garden.

For one second, he stood transfixed with shock and then went hurtling down the stairs and out into the night. Kitty was lying very white and still on the thick, uncut grass of the lawn. Then she moaned faintly.

Lights began to go on in the servants' quarters and the cook was the first to appear. Lord Chesworth shouted to her to

149

send his carriage for the doctor and to fetch blankets. Then he sat down on the lawn beside his half-conscious wife and waited, afraid to touch her or move her in case any of her bones were broken.

The doctor finally arrived and made a quick examination. He ordered the servants to carry Kitty into the house, but Peter Chesworth would let no one else touch his wife.

He paced up and down nervously while the doctor made a thorough examination.

"No bones broken, my Lord," he said with relief. "A bad sprain and a slight concussion. She's a very lucky young lady. If the Misses Dwight-Hammond had had their lawn cut, she might be dead. As it is, the thick, long grass acted as a type of cushion." He gave Kitty a sedative, promised to call in the morning, and took his leave.

Peter Chesworth carried Kitty to his bedroom and sat holding her hand until the sedative began to take effect. Then he went downstairs to meet Lady Mainwaring and the Dwight-Hammond sisters who had just returned from the ball.

"First snakes and now this!" screamed Matilda.

"Snakes!" Peter Chesworth's thin black

brows snapped together. "What snakes?"

The incident of the adders was explained to him. "Let me examine the bloody room," he snapped. "It sounds like some sort of death trap," Jane wailed piteously.

The women followed him into Kitty's bedroom, flinching and jumping at every shadow. Lord Chesworth turned up the gaslight and walked to the window.

The supports holding the wooden balcony had been sawed through. "But there was a man here to repair the house only this evening," wailed Matilda. "I didn't remember asking any man to repair anything but my memory — you know, Jane — I get tired of saying I can't remember things."

They stood looking at each other in shocked silence. Then Lady Mainwaring summed it up in her clear, light voice.

"Well, my dear Baron, who do you think is trying to murder your wife?"

Chapter Six

The police and local magistrate had made their investigation without success and left by the time Kitty felt well enough to make an appearance downstairs.

Jane was fluttering around in great excitement. "Everyone in Hadsea has sent you cards and presents," she exclaimed. "Even Mr. Chambers, the butcher, sent a lovely ham with a heart round it made out of the best pork sausages. Such an imaginative touch. Let me see . . . there is cologne from the chemist, grapes from the greengrocer, and, this gigantic box of chocolates from — why that's strange. There is no card. Maybe it fell out. It could be from the souvenir shop but they have already sent you a pretty box made of shells."

"How kind they all are," said Kitty. "I shall write and thank them all."

Jane looked timidly at the chocolates. "Do you think I could have just one before Matilda comes in?" she pleaded. "I have such a sweet tooth. My husband — who was in fact the Earl of Somerset," she added in a whisper, "always teased me and said I wouldn't have a tooth in my head by the time I was forty. But I have them all!

"Now Matilda says I will get spotty skin even though I haven't a mark on it. But, just one teensy one wouldn't hurt!"

Kitty smiled and started to take off the wrapping. "Of course. You can have as many as you like." She lifted the lid of the box. "Why, there is a letter inside. Now we will know who sent them." Kitty handed Jane the box of chocolates and opened the letter. It was simple and to the point. "Do you know your husband is trying to kill you? A friend."

Kitty dropped it onto her lap and stared at Jane with a white face. But Jane was engrossed in selecting her first chocolate. "Should I take a *hard* center or a soft?" she murmured. "Hard is somehow not so indulgent. Yes . . . yes, I shall take hard."

Kitty escaped from the room, leaving Jane in her chocolate dream. She took the letter to her room and studied it carefully. It was inscribed in block capital letters on cheap paper. It was postmarked London.

Why should her husband wish to kill her? Suddenly, a picture of him dancing with Veronica Jackson came into her mind.

She remembered how Veronica had swayed against him.

Kitty then realized that she did not really know very much about her husband. Surely his sudden passion for her was strange in view of the fact that he had shown little interest in her during their brief engagement. And Kitty was not quite so unsophisticated as she had been then.

There was a scratching at the door and Jane's voice called timidly, "I've brought you the rest of the chocolates, dear Kitty, and a letter from your mother.

"I know it's from your mama," she went on as Kitty opened the door, "because it's got her name on the envelope."

Taking the letter and smiling weakly, Kitty said, "Please do have the chocolates for yourself, Jane. I have such a headache, I must lie down."

"Of course, my dear. But I won't eat them all," said Jane clutching the box. "Just a teensy bit more."

She drifted out and Kitty sat down on the bed and slowly began to open her mother's letter.

It contained only two sentences and the writing was sprawled erratically across the page. "Your husband is an evil man," wrote Mrs. Harrison. "Lady Henley and I saw him at the opera in the company of a Scarlet Woman. You must pray for God's judgment on him and forgive me for the evil I have brought upon you. Your loving Mother."

Kitty put down the letter slowly. She felt sick. Her happiness the night of the ball seemed only a small, bright spot in her memory, with herself and her husband moving in the small camera of her mind like theatrical players. She had endured enough. There was no light and laughter left in the world. It was all a gaudy parade and a sham, peopled with carnival figures. She walked to the window and stared at the summer view sadly, as if she were looking at a childhood photograph. The magic had gone. She would return to London and become the Baroness everyone expected, rude, haughty, and cruel.

Feeling cold and empty, she made her way back downstairs. Peter Chesworth and Lady Mainwaring were waiting for her. Kitty gave them both a thin bright smile and began talking in a cold, flat voice of how much she wished to return to London. Lady Mainwaring tried to tease her back to the old Kitty but without success. She dispensed the teacups with the stiff formality of a dowager.

When Kitty had finally retired for the night and was sitting in bed propped up on the pillows and looking with unseeing eyes at the book on her lap, the door opened and her husband came in.

He gave her an endearing smile and started to take off his jacket.

"Pray, what are you doing?" asked Kitty icily.

Peter Chesworth looked around in surprise. "I'm getting ready for bed, my dear."

"You have your own bedroom," said Kitty flatly. Her voice sounded dull and old.

He looked at her. "I think your accident has shaken you up more than I realized."

"It has perhaps brought me to my senses," said his wife. "You have my money. That is what you married me for, is it not?" He would have spoken but she held up her hand. "No . . . please spare me any more fake protestations of love. You wanted my money, my dear Lord, and that is all you are going to get. I am sure you can satisfy your . . . needs . . . elsewhere. In fact I gather you have already been doing so."

Lord Chesworth flushed an angry red. So she had heard about Veronica Jackson. He opened his mouth to make a withering reply and then closed it again. A strategic retreat would be better.

"I insist you are still suffering from shock, Kitty. We will talk about this further in the morning."

Kitty's hard manner broke. "Oh, just go away and leave me," she said with her voice breaking, and giving her husband more of a guilty stab to the heart than all her anger had done.

He closed the door quietly and went to walk on the beach. Of all the silly things to do, he fumed. To fall in love like a schoolboy with one's own wife. All his amours had been with experienced women. He suddenly felt at a loss and as inexperienced as an adolescent.

The rhythmic sound of the small waves tugging at the shore finally soothed his battered spirits. He had never lacked courage before. He would woo her. That was it! And having decided on a campaign plan, Peter Chesworth took himself off to bed.

The journey to London the next day was a nightmare of suffocating heat as the barometer soared into the nineties. When the train finally steamed into Paddington station, Peter Chesworth breathed a sigh of relief. His wife had sat with her head buried in a book for the whole journey. When they reached the end of the platform, to his horror, Kitty turned and held out her hand to him. "Since you have obviously so many *affairs* to attend to, I am sure you will not mind if I continue my visit with Lady Mainwaring."

He looked at Lady Mainwaring for help but she suddenly seemed to have become enthralled with the mechanics of the steam engine.

"Kitty, this is ridiculous," he expostulated. "We had better go home and talk."

But he addressed the empty, smoky air of the station. His wife was already following the luggage out of the station at a smart pace.

Emily Mainwaring put a hand on his arm. "Something is very wrong, Peter. Please leave it to me to find out what is the matter and I will speak to you tomorrow."

He nodded dumbly and watched their carriage until it was out of sight.

In the carriage, Kitty was giving Lady Mainwaring the benefit of a fund of social small talk, delivered in a hard, bright voice. Suddenly in the middle of an amusing anecdote about Jane Dwight-Hammond's poems, she broke off and buried her head in her gloved hands and sobbed, "Oh,

Emily! What will I do? I'm so miserable."

Lady Mainwaring patted her hand. "Welcome back, Kitty. I thought you had gone forever. We'll have some nice tea when we get home and you can tell me all about it."

Under the willow trees in the garden by the canal, Kitty finally sobbed out the story of the two letters. Emily Mainwaring was shocked and puzzled. "Come now, Kitty. You must remember I have known Peter Chesworth for quite a number of years. He is incapable of trying to murder anyone. But someone is. Our first problem is to make sure you are adequately protected at all times. As for your husband, wait and see what happens. I could have sworn he was in love with you."

"Well, I don't love him," said Kitty childishly. "And so he shall find out. Why, he even took Veronica Jackson around when we were engaged. I wonder how *he* would like it if I started going around with another man?"

Emily looked startled. "Now, Kitty, I'm sure it's not the answer. Look — we are invited to dinner at the Barlowe-Smellies tomorrow. Your husband and Veronica Jackson will both be there —"

"I won't go!" screamed Kitty.

"Of course you'll go and, when you see them together, it will put all this nonsense out of your head. In fact, try to put all these dismal thoughts out of your head right now and think of something absolutely ravishing to wear instead. I never did like Veronica Jackson's style. She's one of those bosomy women who eats and drinks so much, she'll look like a cottage loaf before she's forty — which isn't all that far off."

Kitty looked thoughtfully at the flies dancing over the canal. "Where, by the way, is Mr. Jackson, dead?"

"No, she's divorced. Her husband ran off to the States with a nineteen-year-old American heiress three years ago. She was very bitter about it. She felt that she ought to be able to philander but not he."

"Serves her right," said Kitty, stabbing the point of her parasol into the turf as if it were Veronica Jackson's heart.

"Kitty, Kitty," sighed Emily. "It will just turn out to be a very ordinary social evening at the Barlowe-Smellies and you'll find you have nothing to worry about."

The following evening, Mrs. Barlowe-Smellie would have given anything to agree with her. Her son, Percy, had just pointed

160

out to her that she had invited the Baron's mistress along with his wife.

Mrs. Barlowe-Smellie stared at the guest list in horror, hoping that if she kept on looking at it, it might somehow miraculously change. "Don't you keep up with any of the gossip, Mama?" asked her son.

"Gossip . . . well . . . yes . . . servants, weather, yes . . . mistresses, no . . . assignations . . . bedrooms . . . whispers . . . dear, oh, dear . . . not right . . . tut . . . not right at all," gasped Mrs. Barlowe-Smellie.

"Don't worry," said her energetic son, slapping her on the back. "Cheer up, Mater! Veronica Jackson may be a tart but she knows how to behave in company."

He had reckoned without Veronica's jealousy of Kitty. As a Baroness, Kitty took precedence over the other ladies in the room. Then she had no right to look so slim and ethereal and so damned *virginal*, thought Veronica savagely. And she did not like the way Kitty's husband kept looking at her.

When they were seated at the table, Veronica moved directly to the attack. One of the ladies was complaining about the insolence of a shopgirl in Harridges.

"You should ask Kitty about what goes

on in the minds of little shopgirls," remarked Veronica languidly. "She can give you first-hand information."

Kitty looked Veronica straight in the eyes. "I see you believe the gossip that I was a shopgirl before I was married. That is not true. My father was a stockbroker. The 'shopgirl' came about because of the jealous gossip of some raddled old tart." And flicking Veronica a look of contempt, Kitty picked up her glass of wine and turned to continue her conversation with the gentleman on her right.

Veronica flushed dark red. She had lost round one. She turned to Peter Chesworth and began to carry on a determined flirtation. Kitty had begun to talk of the weather and how she would love to go boating on the Thames. Veronica's eyes flashed and she moved forward for round two.

"Peter, darling," she said in a loud voice with her hand possessively on his arm. "Do you remember that day we spent on the river, floating along under the trees? I shall never forget it."

Once again she was transfixed by Kitty's direct stare.

Kitty's hard, high voice carried round the room. "If you are trying to let me know that you have been carrying on a liaison with my husband, spare your breath. I am well aware of the fact, madame, so you need not try to embarrass me or the rest of the company longer."

Veronica got to her feet in a rage. "Why, you rude little bitch," she hissed.

"I may be rude," said Kitty calmly, "and I may be a bitch, but at least I'm not a silly old tart!"

Veronica burst into noisy tears and ran from the room.

There was a shocked silence, until Mrs. Barlowe-Smellie plunged in, "Treacle tart now . . . sustaining . . . nursery food, of course . . . filling . . . old nanny used to . . . but jam . . . we did love strawberry jam," she finished brightly.

Everyone immediately started talking about nannies. The man on her left whom Kitty identified as Henry . . . oh, dear . . . of the tea party, gave her a wink and said, "I hope you're not always going to be so brutally honest. We'll all be scared to death of you."

"Good," said Kitty in a composed voice, but putting her hands under the table to stop their trembling. In her mind, a punt floated lazily down the Thames on a sunny afternoon and Veronica's voluptuous figure was clasped in Peter Chesworth's arms.

Then she took a clear look at the young man. He was not much older than herself and had very fair hair, thick fair lashes, and blue eyes.

Addicted as she was to black curly hair and pale gray eyes, she realized that Henry . . . oh dear . . . would be considered a very handsome young man by most of the debutantes.

"Do tell me your name," she said, blinding him with a dazzling smile. "Mrs. Barlowe-Smellie introduced you as Henry oh dear and I can't call you that."

He laughed. "I love the way Mrs. Barlowe-Smellie talks. It's as good as a crossword. Great fun filling in the blanks. My name is Henry Dwight-Hammond."

Kitty cried out in surprise. "But I was staying with two sisters of that name at Hadsea only a few days ago."

"My maiden aunts," said Henry. "Are they as batty as ever?"

"Oh, no, they're sweet. I loved them."

"I like them too," said Henry. "If only Jane would stop spouting poems at me. When I was out in South Africa with my regiment, she sent me a poem and I left it lying around the barracks by mistake. I never lived it down. Want to hear it?"

Kitty smiled. "Yes, please."

"Our Henry is out on the veldt
A gun in his hand he heldt
And ever to the fore
He shot the terrible Boer."

Kitty laughed delightedly and then laughed louder as she caught the cold expression on her husband's face.

Henry was charmed by her response. "I say, feel like taking a trip to the zoo with me tomorrow? Oh, I am sorry. I got carried away and forgot you were married."

"Well, if it doesn't bother you, I don't see why it should bother me," said Kitty lightly.

An unidentifiable gleam flickered across Henry's eyes. "Then shall we say one o'clock tomorrow?"

Kitty nodded and smiled and then her attention was caught by the gentleman on her other side.

Peter Chesworth was unable to get a word alone with his wife. Kitty felt that he could have snubbed Veronica's flirting easily. She continued to turn all her charm on Henry Dwight-Hammond.

Emily Mainwaring tried to stop Kitty from going out with Henry unescorted. "Young matrons who make a dead set at a young man, the way you did last night, can have their actions misinterpreted."

"Oh, you're always so cynical," said Kitty. "I want to have a bit of fun. And he likes me."

"I am simply stating the truth," said Lady Mainwaring. "You have blossomed into a very pretty woman. You will find that a lot of young fellows will 'like' you, as you put it, given half a chance."

"Well, I'm going anyway," said Kitty mulishly.

Lady Mainwaring was, after all, a few years older than Kitty's husband and Kitty did so long for the undemanding company of someone her own age.

Henry Dwight-Hammond arrived in a sparkling new motorcar that seemed to seal Lady Mainwaring's disapproval. Motorcars were not quite respectable. Lady Mainwaring belonged strictly to the "carriage class."

But Kitty was thrilled. It was all so exciting and "up-to-date." Up-to-date was the latest slang expression and like most of her contemporaries, Kitty did not want to be thought old-fashioned.

"You are going to the zoo, aren't you?" Emily asked, peering at the motorcar as if it were some strange beast.

Henry flushed. "I thought we might take a little spin down Richmond way."

Lady Mainwaring looked Henry straight in the eyes. "I expect Kitty back not later than six this evening."

"Oh, righty-ho," said Henry blithely. He added to Kitty as they moved off, "She goes on like your mother."

Kitty tossed her head. "I'm so *tired* of old people."

She immediately felt disloyal but it was so jolly to bowl along in a spanking new motorcar, nipping past the disapproving stares of the ladies and gentlemen in their carriages.

They finally stopped at the Star and Garter at Richmond and Henry ushered Kitty out onto the terrace. It was a weekday, so very few people were on the river. Henry ordered champagne for Kitty and whiskey and soda for himself. The river turned and sparkled under the willow trees. A few children were playing "ducks and drakes" at the water's edge, their high, excited screams, blown on the summer breeze, reaching Kitty's ears. They sat in companionable silence for a long time until the tinny tune from a barrel organ down by the river sailed into the air. A drunk man started dancing to the music, his raucous voice floating up to them, mellowed by the distance.

> "Oh, yew are my 'oney, 'oneysuckle,
> I am the bee.
> I'd like ter sip the 'oney
> From those sweet red lips, yer see.
> I luvs yer dearly, dearly,
> And I wants yer ter luv me.
> You are the 'oney, 'oneysuckle,
> I am the bee."

Kitty became aware of a hand on her arm and Henry's whiskey-breath in her ear. "I'd like to sip some honey from your lips, Kitty."

Kitty drew her arm away and stared at Henry in surprise.

He flushed and then said, "Want to go on the river?"

"Oh, yes," said Kitty, clapping her hands in delight. Henry had probably just been singing the words of the song. She couldn't possibly have heard him properly.

He led the way down to the river and helped Kitty into a rowboat and then started rowing swiftly upstream. It was hard-going against the current but Henry was a powerful young man and wanted to get the Baroness away somewhere quiet.

Of course she wouldn't respond to his advances in public.

At last, panting heavily, he moored the boat under the shade of some willows beside a little island. "Shall we sit on the grass for a little?" he asked. Kitty agreed and waited until Henry had spread out a carriage rug on the grass and then she gingerly sat down. Then she jumped in surprise. Henry had removed his jacket, his collar, and his waistcoat. He then flung himself down in the rug beside her and, rolling over, pillowed his head on her lap.

She gazed down transfixed by the red-veined blue eyes that were looking up at her from between their thick, blonde lashes and then suddenly down at her left breast which was being imprisoned by Henry's hand.

She sat quite still, every detail of the scene bright and vivid as if it had been suddenly lit up by a magnesium flare. The green-and-gray river seemed to have stopped flowing and not a breath of air moved the willow trees. Each long blade of grass stood to attention, a kingfisher sat transfixed on his branch over the water, and on the tanned hand spread over her breast, each gold hair stood out sharply like a pig's bristle.

Then a breath of wind like a sigh rippled through the leaves and the kingfisher flashed over the water. Kitty tried to struggle to her feet. "What on earth do you think you are doing?" screamed Kitty.

"What am I doing?" mumbled Henry, feeling dizzy with the combination of whiskey, hot sun, and female proximity. Then he straightened up and said in a louder voice, "I'm bloody well making love to you, that's what. Don't spoil the day by being coy. What else did you expect?"

"I thought we were spending the day together as friends," stammered Kitty.

"Oh, come *on*," said Henry rudely. "A married woman like yourself hands me an open invitation, as it were, in front of her husband, and you expect me to believe you just wanted the pleasure of my company?" He forced her down on the grass and threw a muscular leg over her slim body, excited to discover it was soft and yielding instead of encased in the usual stays.

Mercifully, a party aboard a pleasure launch rounded the bend of the river and started rudely cheering Henry on. Henry released Kitty and cursed the merrymakers on the boat who were gleefully shouting helpful advice.

Kitty saw her chance of escape and took

it. She ran to the rowboat, jumped in, and pushed off. The strong current carried her swiftly downstream away from Henry who was shouting and cursing on the edge of the island. It was then that Kitty realized that the oars were left behind. She settled back in the stern of the boat and resigned herself to her fate, lying back as immobile as the Lady of Shalott and just about as interested in her surroundings.

She sailed past the Star and Garter and was dimly aware of the boatman shouting to her. A stately little figure in one of her high-collared white organza dresses, a white lacy hat, and new white-buttoned boots, Kitty stared straight in front of her, uncaring and unseeing.

Suddenly, a boat hook clamped over the bow jerked her into an awareness of her surroundings. Her rescuers were the men on the pleasure launch and she recoiled from their loud voices and reaching hands. The skipper shoved them aside. "C'mon, miss!" he shouted. "I ain't going to let any of 'em touch you."

Kitty grasped the skipper's hand, was hauled on board, and hustled into the protection of the small wheelhouse, where the skipper seated her on a small stool and slammed the door on the noisy crowd.

She told him in a low voice that the row-boat had escaped from its moorings before Henry could climb aboard and then she blushed painfully as she realized that the skipper must have seen her with Henry on the island. But he merely nodded and puffed away at his pipe. Then he pointed out various landmarks and told her that he would set her down at Blackfriars Pier where she would find a hansom to take her home. From time to time, the leering faces of the increasingly drunken party on board pressed against the windows of the wheelhouse, looking, in the fiery rays of the setting sun, like so many bacchantes staring out of the windows of hell.

The kindly skipper gave her his protection across the pier until she found a hansom and as the cab clopped its way to Regents Park, Kitty felt absolutely miserable and ashamed.

Lady Mainwaring was fortunately in the garden at the back of the house and did not see Kitty's arrival home in the cab. Kitty did not want to see that "I told you so" look on her friend's face and was able to escape to her room and change her soiled dress.

She would have been very annoyed had

she realized that Lady Mainwaring was perfectly aware that something unpleasant had happened, after one look at her strained face. She would have been equally annoyed had she realized that Emily Mainwaring had spent the afternoon discussing her with her husband.

Peter Chesworth was furious about the letters and furious that Kitty had gone off with Henry Dwight-Hammond.

"The man's a positive boor. A callow young pup," he raged. "I'll wait here until my wife gets back and I'll insist she comes straight home with me."

"That won't get you anywhere, Peter," sighed Emily. "Kitty pokers up at the merest hint of bullying. Treat her very gently and she'll come round."

"What about these letters?" asked Lord Chesworth.

"Given time, Kitty will realize that her mother is strange to say the least and that the anonymous letter was simply a piece of spite."

"But someone did try to kill her."

Emily frowned. "I can't think who on earth would want to, Peter. But Hadsea is a small place and you still get a lot of inbreeding in these country retreats. The local idiot probably had a brainstorm."

"But it does not have to be a local," protested Peter. "It could be anyone."

He frowned suddenly and ran his long fingers through his black hair. "Do you think Henry Dwight-Hammond is enough protection?"

"No, I do not!" said Lady Mainwaring roundly. "And I think Kitty needs protection from *him*. I sent Judson, my footman, to follow them. He'll keep up with them easily. A good horse is still the equal of any of these tin-pot motorcars any day. Are you going to the Hallidays' midnight supper? Good, then I'll bring Kitty and you can continue your courtship."

When Kitty was in her rooms changing, a breathless Judson burst in on Lady Mainwaring with the tale of Kitty's voyage.

"Why didn't you take a boat out after them?" snapped Lady Mainwaring.

The poor footman explained that there had not been another one available. He had waited on the pier and the next thing he had known, Kitty flashed past him, alone in the boat. He had ridden down to the next point of access on the river but she had disappeared.

Emily told him of Kitty's safe return and then sat staring at the canal, deep in thought. Obviously Kitty must be much more closely guarded. At least, she thought grimly, today would have taught her a lesson.

She had not counted on the resilience of youth. By the time they had arrived at the Hallidays' place on the Thames, Kitty was remembering more about the jealous look on her husband's face when she had flirted with Henry, than the sequel. Henry was mercifully absent from the party but her mother and Lady Henley were present. They sat under one of the huge oak trees in the garden, Lady Henley staring at her plate and Mrs. Harrisen staring out across the water. Mrs. Harrison looked up as her daughter came over to join them. "My poor, poor child," she exclaimed. "I'm all right, Mama," said Kitty crossly.

Everyone attending the party had been asked to come dressed in white but there was something about the blinding, unrelieved white of her mother's ensemble which teetered on the thin edge of madness. Even her long beads, which she kept plucking at, were white and she had whitened her face with too much powder. Lady Henley raised her massive head from the trough of food in front of her. "Going to take a walk with Kitty," she announced, ponderously, getting to her feet and laying a pudgy hand on Kitty's arm. "Come and look at the flowers," she said, leading Kitty out of earshot.

She came to an abrupt stop behind a bank of rhododendrons. "It's about your mama, Kitty. She's been drinking rather a lot."

Kitty turned wide eyes on Lady Henley. "But I've never seen her staggering or behaving like a drunk," she protested.

"No," agreed Lady Henley, "and I don't think you will. I'll swear that woman's got a hose in her left boot the way she packs it away. But one minute she's all calm and dreamy and vague and the next she's throwing temper tantrums. She thinks the Boers have got spies all over London and she keeps trying to get policemen to arrest the most innocent people. Then she fumes on about lechers and nasty men and blames herself over and over again for your marriage."

Kitty opened her mouth to reply when she saw the tall figure of her husband standing at the entrance to the garden. She started forward and then saw that Veronica Jackson had reached Peter first and was standing with her hand on his arm.

Feeling a lump of ice forming in her

stomach, Kitty turned away and heard the rest of Lady Henley's story through a fog of misery. "Doctor called . . . take time . . . rest . . . fresh air . . . seaside . . . won't go . . . don't know what to do."

"Well, I don't know what to do either," said Kitty heartlessly. Her own problem loomed so large, she could find no room in her heart for anything else.

The buffet beckoned. With a shrug, Lady Henley lumbered off, lured by the irresistible sight of a plate of lobster patties.

Kitty heard a voice at her ear. "What are you doing here, Baroness, alone and palely loitering?"

She turned and found herself face to face with a tall, willowy young man dressed in a white-velvet jacket and sporting a green carnation. He had a large pear-shaped face, a spoiled child's mouth, and very bushy eyebrows.

"I'm communing with nature," said Kitty acidly.

"But how sensible!" he said enthusiastically. "You probably don't remember my name. I was at your wedding. I'm Charlie Styles."

"What a peculiar-colored flower in your buttonhole," said Kitty.

"I wear it in memory of Oscar."

"A friend of yours?" asked Kitty. He looked so sad.

"He was a friend of the world," exclaimed Charlie Styles. "I speak of Mr. Wilde, the greatest poet and playwright of them all."

He looked around at the guests with contempt. "Do you know what he called this lot? This fox-hunting lot, I mean. The unspeakable in full pursuit of the uneatable. But since we're at a supper party, *I* call them — the unspeakable in pursuit of the eatable."

Kitty did not find this sally particularly witty but the young man had such comical eyebrows that she burst out laughing.

"Ah, my dear young lady, I see our souls are in accord," said Mr. Styles, drawing her arm though his. "Shall we promenade and survey the English society animal at play?"

Very much intrigued, Kitty moved off with him. "Look at them all," said Mr. Styles, waving a plump white hand around the gathering. "How foreign! How strange! Do you ever feel alone when you are in a crowd?"

"Oh, yes, indeed!" exclaimed Kitty, much struck, and remembering how foreign she had felt with both the Thackerays and the Pugsleys.

"Good!" said Mr. Styles. "We shall talk some more."

In another part of the garden, Peter Chesworth was talking to Emily Mainwaring. "Who is that most peculiar young man with my wife?"

Emily Mainwaring glanced over to where Kitty and Mr. Styles were walking. "Oh, dear, she's got hold of I'm-always-alone-in-a-crowd, Charlie Styles. Don't worry, he's harmless. Very," she added enigmatically.

The couple was moving toward them and Peter Chesworth started forward to join his wife and found, to his irritation, that that possessive hand of Veronica's was on his arm again.

"What is it, Veronica?" he asked, looking down at her and wondering how she had ever managed to arouse any passion in him whatsoever.

Veronica tugged him away from Emily. "Do you remember what you said that night?" she hissed in his ear.

"What night?" asked Peter, straining to hear what his wife was saying.

"Why — your *wedding* night," said Veronica, her long nails digging into his arm.

"You must come for tea with me tomorrow, dear Kitty," Mr. Styles was saying.

"You said if Kitty were dead, you would marry me," whispered Veronica.

"Eh, what? Yes, yes, of course," said Peter, not hearing a word. What on earth did Kitty see in that effeminate fool?

Now both couples met. Veronica's blue eyes held a glitter of triumph that Kitty did not like. She stared coldly at Veronica's clutching hand and Peter Chesworth suddenly realized that Veronica still had hold of his arm. To jerk it away would seem rude. He smiled at his wife instead. "I've found an excellent table for us over by the water," he said, moving toward her.

"Why that is marvelous, Peter," said Veronica. "Let's grab it right away before someone else gets it. Do excuse us, Kitty. We appear to have interrupted a *fascinating* conversation."

Mr. Styles bowed. "Our souls are in communion," he said, leading Kitty off in a surprisingly strong grip. Kitty felt suddenly that she would like a good cry and Peter Chesworth did not know whether he wanted to strangle Veronica or shoot Mr. Styles. Well, he would take the opportunity to finish things with Veronica, once and for all.

When they sat down at their table, he took Veronica's hand in his and leaned forward to try to firmly, but tactfully, explain to her that he was in love with his wife.

"Look . . . this is awfully difficult. You know I care for you Veronica and always will, but —"

"What ineffable twaddle!" a voice like a newly-honed razor cut across his speech.

It was Mrs. Harrison, glaring down at them with glittering eyes. Then she started to scream. "You whore, you slut, you scarlet woman! And as for you, you —" Like some massive keeper, Lady Henley appeared and drew Mrs. Harrison away.

"You see what I mean, Peter?" sobbed Veronica. "The sooner we sort out this terrible situation, the better." And she got to her feet and fled toward the house.

Meanwhile, Kitty was making arrangements to have tea with Mr. Styles on the following day. "Don't expect anything too grand," he said. "I have diggings with a chap in Sloane Square, Bertie Longfield — jolly good sort. He'll simply adore you. In fact I'll invite some of my other friends to meet you. You are lonely, I can see that."

Kitty warmed to the understanding in his voice. "I would love to meet your friends. Yes. I *am* very lonely," she added loudly, for the benefit of her husband who happened to be within earshot.

The rest of the evening seemed, to Peter Chesworth, to be like some macabre dance with his wife eluding him with all the expertise of a principal of the Covent Garden ballet. What incredible bores these people were! How disgustingly loud and grasping Veronica had become! And any young man who wore a green carnation should be put up in front of a firing squad and shot!

"I'm looking for Kitty," said Lady Mainwaring. "Is she still with Styles?"

"Yes, she is," snapped Lord Chesworth. "Want to do a bit more manipulating and intriguing? Well, she's over there if you want to go wind her key." With that he sought out his hostess and thanked her for a delightful evening in a tone of voice which turned the compliment into an insult, called for his carriage, and went off to his club where — thank God — no pesky women were allowed in.

Mr. Styles's conversation seemed to lose some of its charm for Kitty as soon as her husband had disappeared, but the idea of making her own appointments and having her own friends was novel and exciting. Assuring Mr. Styles that she would see him at three o'clock the following afternoon, she took her leave with a disapproving Emily Mainwaring.

"I suppose it's no use me wasting my breath telling you not to go tomorrow," she remarked in the carriage on the way home.

"No — none at all," said Kitty.

"Oh, well," sighed Lady Mainwaring. "At least you won't get raped."

Chapter Seven

Kitty rang the bell beside a neat white card marked Styles & Longfield on the door of a red, sandstone building in Sloane Square. The door opened and a very small girlish-looking man held out his hand. "I'm Bertie Longfield. I'm afraid Charlie was called away to see a sick aunt but his sister is acting as hostess. Do come in."

He ushered Kitty into a small sitting room. Three elegant young men languidly got to their feet. Bertie made the introductions and said that Charlie's sister, Charlotte, would be along directly.

The door opened and Charlotte sailed in. She looked remarkably like her brother except that her hair was brassy-blonde and she had a high falsetto voice.

"Such a charming little bird of paradise has flown among us. Hasn't she, dear boys? *Charming.* Love your teagie. Do sit down, darling and have some darling, darling cakes. So delicate, aren't they? Like the sunlight on angels' wings."

"Quite," replied Kitty faintly.

"Love, love, *love* the drooping lines of your teagie, absolutely deevie. Beardsley, that's it! Quintessence of Beardsley. Don't you agree, darling boys?"

The darling boys were rolling around the room in fits of the giggles. Kitty began to be annoyed. The room was stuffy and overcrowded with all sorts of irritating bits and bobbles. Heavy blinds sealed off the summer sunshine and cast a pale light upon a large portrait of a nude of indeterminate sex which hung above the fireplace.

Kitty was reminded of a time in the schoolroom when her dress had been unfastened at the back and, instead of telling her about it, the other girls had sniggered all day. She decided it was time the new Kitty took over. A faint look of hauteur settled on her young face. "What are you all sniggering about?" she demanded in a high clear voice.

The giggling stopped. The bevy of young men looked at each other helplessly. "Oh, don't mind them," said Charlotte. "Boys will be boys, I always say."

"How unoriginal of you," said Kitty sweetly. "What for example do you *not* usually say. I'm sure it must be something *very* witty."

To her surprise, the young men burst out

185

in a sort of Greek chorus of "Oh, naughty, naughty. Claws in! Claws in!"

Kitty stared at them in surprise. A little light began to dawn. "Mr. Styles is a devotee of Mr. Oscar Wilde. Are you all perhaps of the . . . same . . . religion, shall we say?"

There was a stunned silence. The innocent, naive child of the middle classes that Charlie Styles had promised them, was turning out to be as formidable as a dowager.

"Oh, do have a cake," said the much-flustered Charlotte. She bent over the tea table and a corner of her dress caught on her chair and lifted up to expose a length of black, hairy, muscular leg encased in a black sock and suspenders. Charlotte Styles was Charlie after all. Blazing with fury inside but keeping a calm, social smile on her face, Kitty got to her feet and insisted on taking her leave.

"Do not trouble yourself, Charlotte. I can see myself out," said Kitty. As she reached the door, she raised the point of her lacy parasol and, watched by a horrified audience, she neatly lifted "Charlotte's" blond wig from his head and threw it into the fireplace.

Charlie Styles burst into tears. "Get

out!" he screamed, his face like an anguished clown's, as the tears mixed with paint and powder coursed down his cheeks.

Kitty took several deep breaths when she reached the street. She decided to take the underground railway home in the hope that the novel experience would take away some of the nightmare of the afternoon.

She bought a ticket at Sloane Square station and went down the steps to the platform which was surely unusually crowded. As she waited in the press, a portly man told her that a train had broken down but that the line was now clear and another train would be through any minute. "I've never traveled underground before," confided Kitty.

"Oh, I'm used to it," said her portly friend. "But m' daughter — she's about your age — gets very excited. Here . . . if you move a little to the front, you'll see the train coming along the track."

Kitty leaned forward but all she could see was the black mouth of the tunnel. Then she heard a faint rumbling sound and the ground began to tremble under her feet. "That's it now," she cried. "I can hear it coming."

She turned her head to smile at her new

friend and received a vicious shove on the back which sent her sailing onto the tracks. Everyone started screaming at once and Kitty saw the lights of the train bearing down upon her. Suddenly a man was beside her on the tracks. He lifted her bodily, threw her like a rag doll onto the platform, and then leaped to safety himself as the train thundered into the station. It was Judson, Lady Mainwaring's footman.

Kitty was so terrified and flustered and dizzied by the anxious faces, that she would have allowed herself to be swept onto the train with the crowd, but Judson held her back. "This is a matter for the police, my Lady," he said.

She put a trembling hand to her brow. "The police, Judson?"

"Wot's all this 'ere?" said an authoritative voice. Judson explained, the policeman took out his notebook, and everyone began to talk at once. It had been a little fellow with a scar, it had been an old lady in a big hat, it had been that fat man over there. Kitty's new friend explained that he had been standing beside her when she fell but that he had not seen who had pushed her. Kitty, Judson, and the most coherent of the witnesses were led off to Chelsea police station where they spent a confusing hour making statements and getting nowhere.

The inspector settled the babble. If my Lady would go home, then a gentleman from Scotland Yard would call on her as soon as possible.

Lady Mainwaring was very worried when she heard the news about the latest attempt on Kitty's life. The sooner the girl's marriage was settled the better. Emily Mainwaring, who had always considered herself a sympathizer with the agitators for women's emancipation, now suddenly wished Kitty would get pregnant. That would settle her down. Nothing like a nursery full of children to keep her out of mischief. She told Kitty to go and relax in the garden and sent a messenger off to find Lord Peter Chesworth.

The light was fading over the city as Kitty sat at the edge of the canal and wondered who was trying to kill her. Perhaps the incidents were not related at all. The incident at Hadsea could simply have been a practical joke that had gone too far. And the press on the platform at Sloane Square underground station had been so great, someone could have lunged against her by accident.

She was suddenly aware of someone

walking across the grass toward her and turned her head sharply. It was her husband, the expression on his face unreadable in the dimming light. He sat down next to her without a word and they both stared straight ahead at the glassy waters of the canal. The orange glow that was nighttime London began to spread across the sky and the ever-present hum of the great city reached their ears, faintly. Some wild animal roared in his cage in the nearby zoo and the sharp clop of a horse's hoofs on the street outside the house only served to punctuate the stillness of the evening.

Kitty slid her eyes sideways and studied her husband's profile, the high-bridged nose, the hooded eyes, and the long, thin, mobile mouth. He suddenly turned and looked at her and she blushed.

"My dear," he said, "this situation is ridiculous. Your life is in danger and I feel I should have some right to protect you."

"You have no right," said Kitty in such a low voice that he had to strain to hear.

He studied his wife's averted profile for a minute and then began. "Before I met you, I was having an affair with a certain lady, I think you know that."

"Yes," whispered Kitty.

"That is all very definitely over."

Now Kitty jerked her head around. "Over! It certainly doesn't look like it."

"I have tried to explain matters to the lady but she is . . . well . . . very possessive. I'm sorry about it, Kitty. Will you forgive me? Our marriage has had such a bad start. I feel sure we could make something of it if only we tried a little. Will you come home with me?"

He rested his arm along the back of her chair without touching her but she felt as if an electric shock had been passed through her body. She sat very still, her face unreadable in the gathering dark.

He went on, his voice hesitating slightly. "I have not been, by any means, a saint, Kitty. I have had a lot of experience with . . . well . . . experienced women. I have never had to . . . court a young girl like yourself and I find myself somewhat at a loss and that makes me behave in a somewhat boorish manner at times."

Still his wife kept silent.

"I heard you say the other night that you were lonely. Well, I am lonely too, in a certain way. At the moment, all that I am asking you for is companionship. I will not . . . share your bed until we have perhaps reached a certain understanding.

"I was worried sick about losing

Reamington. A lot of the chaps in my position marry heiresses and, like a fool, I did not realize that I was also responsible for another human being. I thought you would go your way and I'd go mine. But I hate it when you go away, Kitty. Please come home with me."

It had cost Peter Chesworth a great deal to make this speech and suddenly he realized that if she rejected him, he would feel like an utter fool. His wife gave a little sigh and he suddenly burst out, "Oh, for God's sake, can't you open your bloody mouth?"

The instant it was out, he could have bitten off his tongue but his wife gave a low gurgle of laughter. "Now *that* sounds more like the husband I know. Yes, Peter, I will come back with you on those terms. Goodness knows, I have been getting into some terrible messes. I had better tell you about them because I've discovered that society gossip is faster than Marconi any day."

She began to tell her husband about her adventures with Henry and then of her visit to Charlie Styles. At first she began quietly and sorrowfully but finally the idiocy of both adventures struck her and she began to laugh. Peter laughed with her, particularly at the tale of Charlie Styles's wig but he inwardly decided to give Henry Dwight-Hammond a bloody nose at the first opportunity.

Gratified to find that her aristocratic husband was not going to call her a naive fool and that he, on the contrary, was the first person that had ever really listened to her, Kitty went on to tell him about the evening at the Pugsleys. He laughed heartily at the story of Mr. Pugsley's new suspenders but stopped when Kitty began to tell him about little Jane Pugsley's "imaginings" of a hand at the window setting fire to the curtains. He would have put it down to a child's vivid imagination had it not been for the subsequent attempts on Kitty's life.

Peter closed his long fingers around Kitty's little hand. "You need not be frightened again, my dear. We will go everywhere together."

Kitty looked down at the hand clasping hers. She was held rigid in a sea of ecstatic emotion as little waves of feeling lapped through her body. All thoughts of her handsome husband being a murderer fled into the dark corners of the summer evening. Kitty sat as still as a statue, frightened to move and break the spell, quite unaware that her highly sophisticated husband was experiencing the same emotions.

Peter Chesworth was fascinated that this slight physical contact with this young girl — his wife — could hold him imprisoned in a stronger current of passion than he had ever felt before during the most intimate contact with other women.

Both of them sat, rapt and enchanted, almost painfully aware of every sight and scent in the dark summer's night. A clump of delphiniums blazed in the darkness like a blue flame, a single ripple snaked across the canal like a brush stroke in a Chinese painting and the tinny music from a party in one of the nearby houses sounded infinitely poignant. The smells of cooking from the kitchens — wine, onions, fresh bread, and herbs — mingled with the heady scents of the flowers in the garden.

Lady Mainwaring took one step into the garden, looked at the silent figures by the water and retreated into the house. How odd to think that she had sat just like that one summer's evening long ago with a young man who was to become her husband. Emily sighed. All that magic of youth and love fleeing before the humdrum daily routine of marriage, turning the tremulous young girl into a brittle sophisticate and the young man into a middle-aged eccentric, dying of diphtheria contracted in a London slum, because his pride had been hurt.

Past forgotten and future unheeded, the enchanted couple sat on, mute, their hands still clasped. Then there was a discreet cough behind them and the evening shattered like fragile glass. Kitty became aware of a cramp in her leg and Lord Chesworth noticed that a large beetle was crawling across the garden table.

"A person from Scotland Yard to see you, my Lady," said the butler. "I have put him in the study."

"That'll be about what happened this afternoon in the underground," said Kitty, getting to her feet. "Do come with me."

But the detective from Scotland Yard said, firmly and politely, that he would like to see the Baroness alone. Lord Chesworth opened his mouth to protest but Kitty smiled at him so warmly and said, "I am sure it will only take a minute, Peter, and then we can go home," that he merely shrugged and left the room.

The detective introduced himself as Mr. Albert Grange. At first sight, he was an unprepossessing man. He had a round, fat, middle-aged face embellished with a tired mustache and thin strands of hair carefully arranged on the top of his head to conceal as much of his baldness as possible. His grubby, high, celluloid collar was cutting into his jowls and his dark gray suit showed shiny patches of wear. But his little brown eyes were twinkling with intelligence and he had a fatherly manner that was very endearing.

"Well, my Lady," he said, "I'm blessed if I know where to begin. How's about you beginning at the beginning and telling me about everything in your own words. Now, there's no one in the room but you and me and I'm not going to take notes. So just you talk away about every little bit that you can think of."

"It all started at Hadsea," said Kitty.

Mr. Grange interrupted. "No . . . start before Hadsea. Before you was married would be a good beginning."

For the second time that evening, Kitty had found a good listener. She told more than she knew. The astute Mr. Grange quickly grasped that her mother had arranged the marriage but he said nothing until Kitty had reached the end of her story.

Then Mr. Grange asked in a deceptively mild voice, "You don't suspect your husband, now, do you?"

"Of course not," Kitty nearly screamed and then calmed herself. "Why should I?"

"Well, now. You're a very wealthy young lady by all accounts."

"But he has my money. I — I — mean, my m-money is his," stammered Kitty.

Mr. Grange looked at her thoughtfully. "You must pardon me, my Lady, if my questions seem impertinent, but money breeds more crime than anything — next to passion that is. We get lots of these here creem passionellies down at the Yard. But in this case, there's no question of another lady, now?"

Kitty thought of Veronica Jackson. He had said it was over. She must trust him.

"No — none at all, and may I suggest, Mr. Grange, that we look for someone else. I do love my husband, you see." Her voice broke a little on the last sentence and Mr. Grange took mental note. Loves her husband all right, he thought cynically, but that isn't the problem. The problem is — does he love her or that Mrs. Jackson he's been seen around with? But he felt he had gone far enough.

He tried another tack. "What about this Lady Henley. You say your mother got in touch with her by advertising in the *Times*.

197

Can you imagine, just imagine, mind, that this Lady Henley would want to kill you?"

Kitty giggled. "Not unless she's turned cannibal. She isn't interested in anything but food."

"Well, then, has anyone shown you any bit of dislike or hate that you can think of?"

Kitty thought of the screaming, crying Charlie Styles but to explain it to the detective would send Charlie and his friends to prison. Then there was Veronica. But that would mean betraying her husband's trust. She shook her head.

"Well, my Lady, that leaves us pretty much where we started. Now if I could just take you through it all again. . . ."

It was two hours later when the detective decided he had gotten as much as he was going to get that evening. "I'll call on your mother and Lady Henley tomorrow," he said. "Now, if you would just tell his Lordship to step in here for a few minutes . . ."

Kitty found her husband pacing up and down the hall outside. "Of course I'll see him," he said when she relayed her message. "And I'll get rid of him quickly. Insufferable little bounder. Go and see to your packing."

But Kitty was not to learn what passed

198

between the detective and her husband. Peter Chesworth was very silent on the road home and Kitty desperately wished he would say something to raise the cloud from her mind. For the detective's insinuations had started her worrying again. What did she know, after all, of this strange man sitting next to her?

He seemed to brighten, however, when they reached their town house. He sent Checkers, the butler, to fetch the decanter of sherry and ushered her into the drawing room. Kitty looked at Checkers's fat retreating back and when he had closed the door on them, she asked her husband, "Did you hire the servants, Peter? They are not at all like the ones at Reamington."

"No, why?" said Peter. "Your mother engaged the staff here. If you don't like any of them, get rid of them."

Kitty quailed before the idea of giving the slab-faced Checkers notice. "Perhaps it's because I am not used to many servants," she ventured. "I will wait a few days."

The door opened abruptly and Checkers entered bearing the tray. He turned his back on Peter as he deferentially handed Kitty her glass. She glanced up into his watery eyes and started at the look of undisguised venom on his fat white face. In a second it was gone, leaving her to think that she must be overtired and imagining things.

After they had finished their drinks, Peter escorted his wife to the door of her bedroom. He bent his head and kissed her lightly on the cheek but her body was so soft and pliant against his and that scent from her hair — gardenia, that was it — was clouding his senses. His mouth slid across her cheek and found her mouth and Kitty's mind went spiraling off into a dark, dark night lit by bursts of fireworks. Then, gradually, as if it were happening to someone else, she became aware of long, hard fingers stroking her bosom and a lean muscular leg pressing between her thighs. Bright-colored images chased each other across the night of her mind. The sun sparkling on the blond hairs on Henry's hand as it clutched her breast, Charlie's blond wig lying in the fireplace, and the white body of her husband, gleaming in the electricity as he laughed at her picture. She went rigid and cold as if someone had thrown a bucket of water over her. Peter was immediately aware of her reaction and cursed himself for getting carried away. He kissed her lightly on the forehead and with a husky "good night" took himself off to his own room.

Immediately, Kitty wanted him back. Not to hold her like that in that frightening way but just . . . she wanted . . . oh, what in the name of heaven did she want! Kitty threw herself on her bed and indulged in a much-needed bout of tears.

Kitty shyly entered the breakfast room next morning but the passionate lover of the night before was immersed in the *Daily Telegraph* and merely smiled at her and returned to his paper.

At last he put it down and turned his attention to his breakfast. "Good God," he exclaimed, lifting cover after cover. "This all looks as if it had been made a week ago. Checkers, who on earth is our cook?"

"Mrs. Checkers," replied the butler blandly.

"Your wife, eh? Well you'd better straighten her out this morning, Kitty."

Again that look from Checkers, a mixture of insolence and venom, was directed at Kitty. But this time her husband intercepted it.

"Checkers, you're dismissed. You've got your marching orders. Now go, and take your wife with you. Your wages will be forwarded to you," snapped Peter Chesworth.

The butler opened his mouth to say something and was forestalled.

"You want to know the reason, I suppose," said Peter Chesworth. "Well, I'm dismissing you for dumb insolence and not because of your wife's hellish cooking. Not another word. Go."

The butler hesitated but Peter Chesworth was again reading his paper and Kitty realized that her husband did not doubt for a minute that his order would be disobeyed. Nor was it. Checkers finally choked out, "Very good, my Lord," and closed the door quietly behind him.

Peter Chesworth threw down his paper again. "I'm dashed if I know what's going on. Because of all this marriage mess — sorry, Kitty — I never really *looked* at any of the servants. I'd better run around to Scotland Yard and get that detective of yours onto Checkers. I've never seen anyone with such a vile look. Why, he looked as if he could have murdered you," he added cheerfully.

Kitty shuddered. "I was going to have luncheon with Mama today and I wondered if you would join me?"

Her husband looked at her in dismay.

"Can't do it, my dear. I have a luncheon appointment in the city with a chap who's getting me a special deal on a cart-load of superphosphates."

His wife looked puzzled and Peter laughed. "I forget you don't know about farming. Well, it's one of our farms at Reamington. Jezzald, the farmer, has been overstocking and he doesn't even care. He's taken the heart out of the land until it's good for nothing. Tell you what, I'll drop you off at your mother's and then pick you up afterward. Then my agent had better come over and get rid of this lot of servants and get us some more."

"Oh, but that's heartless!" cried Kitty. "Some of them might not deserve to lose their jobs."

"You'll lose your life by one of them if we're not careful," said her husband grimly. "Don't worry, my agent will sort through their references." There was a slight noise outside the door.

He leaped to his feet but whoever had been in the hallway was gone.

At midday, he escorted Kitty to Park Lane and helped her down from the carriage and bent gallantly to kiss her gloved hand. Kitty looked down at the black, curly head bent over her hand and began to stammer, "P-Peter, I would like to t-tell you . . ." and then lost her courage. She desperately wanted to explain why she had rejected his lovemaking the night before but standing in the middle of the pavement with the coachman within earshot, she felt suddenly shy of the tall stranger who was her husband.

"I just wanted . . . to know . . . that is, when will you be finished with your luncheon?"

"Oh, not very long. Less than two hours if the traffic in the city isn't too heavy. Is that what you really wanted to say?" The pale gray eyes looked uncomfortably shrewd.

"N-no," said Kitty. "But I'll tell you later."

He watched her slight figure walk up the steps and then sprang into the carriage and directed the coachman to drive to the city.

Lady Henley was waiting alone. "Your mama is not feeling very well," she said. "She's gone to lie down. Don't know what's the matter. She was all right this morning. Quite her usual old self. Then she had a sort of faint turn. Anyway, I've ordered a light luncheon for the pair of us."

The luncheon was indeed light by Lady Henley's standards — only five courses with a different wine for each course. Kitty began to feel quite light-headed towards the end. Usually, she was very careful and only drank a little but Lady Henley had proved to be an unusually entertaining companion when she put her mind to it and Kitty found that she had absent-mindedly been draining each glass.

"Where did you say your husband was?" asked Lady Henley.

"He's gone to buy a load of phosphates for one of the farms at Reamington."

Lady Henley grunted. "That's Peter Chesworth all over. When he was in Afghanistan with my son —" She paused. "Didn't you know your husband used to be in the army?"

Kitty shook her head. "Well, what a strange couple you are to be sure," said Lady Henley. "Peter was a Captain in the Wiltshires and a very brave soldier. But my poor son, John, caught a bullet and died in the hospital in Peshawar and Peter got a nasty case of enteric fever and was sent home.

"John used to write to me a lot about Peter. Peter was his Captain. John used to say Peter would dream of nothing but

Reamington. His father was alive at the time and drinking and gambling the estate into rack and ruin. 'I'll save Reamington!' Peter used to tell my son. 'Even if I have to sell my soul to do it!' "

Lady Henley saw the distress on Kitty's face. "Don't take it to heart, my dear. I don't think you realize how much his land means to a man like Peter Chesworth. He loves every stick and stone, man, woman, and child on his estate. He's a good landlord and God knows, there ain't many of that kind of old aristocracy left. He'll expect you to look after his people too. You'll need to see that John on the home farm is going to the dentist and that Molly in the village is attending school and that Jane is marrying the right man and that the old people have enough to eat. All that kind of thing. You didn't just marry Peter Chesworth, you married all these other people y' see. But have your fun in London first because it's a lot of work."

Kitty suddenly remembered Checkers. She told Lady Henley about her husband getting rid of the servants. "Very odd," commented Lady Henley. "But your mama got quite uppity with me. Wanted to get them herself. Probably went to some riff-raff agency."

The dessert was served — a bowl of *chartreuse de pèches à la Reine Alexandra* — and Lady Henley let out a grunt of pure pleasure. "Goody. M' favorite," she explained.

"I don't think I can eat any more," said Kitty faintly.

Lady Henley's eyes glistened. In an effort to do right by her young guest, she had restrained her gluttony. But enough was enough. She drew the bowl toward her and wolfed the whole confection down, gave a hearty, satisfied belch, and called for a plate of *petits fours*. "Don't think I'll bother about a savory today," she remarked, shoving *petits fours* into her mouth with amazing rapidity. The little biscuits had been served in a basket made of intricately spun and woven toffee. Lady Henley picked it up and gave it a baffled look and then, with an almost apologetic glance at Kitty, clamped her jaws around the handle of the basket and started to crunch happily, like a dog with a delicious bone. Slivers of toffee flew right and left and the room was silent except for Lady Henley's massive crunchings.

Kitty began to feel dizzy with the amount of food and wine she had consumed. "I think I'll need to get some fresh air, Lady Henley," she said, rising and clutching the back of her chair for support.

"I'll take you for a drive in the park," said Lady Henley, heaving herself to her feet and ringing for the carriage.

The fresh air did wonders for Kitty. She felt alive and happy and inclined to burst into fits of giggles at the sight of a woman in a large hat or an organ grinder's monkey. Lady Henley felt her eyes beginning to close, glad that her young friend seemed to be in spirits. A snore from her companion sent Kitty into gales of laughter and the astonished stares from the people in the other carriages in the Row made her laugh even harder. The world around her dizzied, sparkled and whirled like bubbles in a champagne glass. She felt like dancing. She *would* dance! She called on the coachman to stop and before he knew what she was about, she had nipped smartly down from the carriage and started dancing away among the other carriages, her frothy skirts sailing about her. With an oath, the coachman told the footman to "get to their heads" and ran after the dancing girl. Carriages stopped, lorgunettes were raised in amazement.

Voices cried, "I say, isn't that Lady Chesworth?"

How delicious it all was! Kitty did a particularly fancy pirouette to the enchanting music singing in her head and bumped up against a stationary carriage. She found herself staring into the horrified eyes of her husband. Beside him sat Veronica Jackson, gleefully surveying her from head to toe.

Peter's carriage had been stopped by Veronica at the corner of Park Lane. Would he mind driving her to the park? She was to meet a friend there. It would only take a minute. When they reached the park, she kept craning her head to look for the mysterious friend and Peter Chesworth had just decided that the friend did not exist when he looked down and saw his wife.

Kitty glared straight at Veronica and the champagne bubble burst. "Get out of that carriage and leave my husband alone," said Kitty. Her voice had carried and the fashionable throng seemed to stop their carriages as one.

"Oh, go away," hissed Veronica. "You're drunk!"

"Get down from that carriage now . . . you *damned* harpy."

Veronica trembled artistically against

Peter. "Darling, can't you *do* something with her?"

That was the final straw. Kitty seized Veronica by the arm and gave it a mighty tug. Veronica pulled back and then made the mistake of standing up. Kitty caught at her dress and gave another heave and Veronica tumbled over headlong onto the grass. There were loud cheers from several of the young men in the carriages around. Cursing, Peter Chesworth jumped to the ground to help Veronica to her feet. She immediately fell heavily against him and put her arms around his neck.

Peter was trying to ease her away from him and avoid the rain of blows descending on his head from Kitty's parasol. Lady Henley's coachman came panting up and Peter almost shoved Veronica into his arms. He then seized his enraged wife and carried her bodily into the carriage. "Drive on, man!" he yelled to his coachman. Kitty had begun to sob hysterically. Her hair was falling down and she had dust and dirt on her skirts from where they had whirled and brushed against the various carriages.

By the time they had reached Hyde Park corner, Kitty was sobbing quietly and by the time they reached home, she was fast asleep. He carried her up the stairs and laid her gently on her bed. He rang the bell for the maid. No reply. He left Kitty sleeping and ran quickly down the stairs to the servants' quarters. Not a soul in sight.

There was a rumble of carriages outside and then a knock at the door. To Peter Chesworth's relief it turned out to be an army of servants from Reamington, headed by the efficient agent, Bryson.

Mr. Bryson shook his head when Peter explained the situation. "I'm sure I don't know where Mrs. Harrison got those servants from. I can't find out anything about any of them."

Peter scribbled out a report on the disappearance of the servants and sent Bryson around to Scotland Yard with it. Then he took himself off to visit Mrs. Harrison.

Mrs. Harrison was lying on a chaise longue in the drawing room at Park Lane. She seemed composed and normal and could give him no help over the matter of the servants. "All I can tell you is that I went to Beechman's Agency and ordered all the servants. The agency promised to forward me their references but they never arrived." She gave him the address of the agency in Shoreditch and leaned back and closed her eyes.

"You must forgive me, Peter, but my doctor recommends quiet and rest. I cannot speak to you further."

Peter Chesworth took his leave and hailed a passing four-wheeler and gave the cabby the address in Shoreditch. It turned out to be an unprepossessing back street and, where the agency should have been, was a fire-blackened gap in the buildings. A slatternly woman nursing her baby on a nearby doorstep volunteered the information that the fire had taken place the previous week but whether there had been an agency there or not she couldn't remember. He received much the same reply up and down the street and eventually gave up and decided to leave the rest of the inquiries to Scotland Yard.

When he returned home, he found that his wife was awake but looking pale and sick. She complained of a blinding headache and her eyes kept filling with tears of remorse as she remembered her behavior in the park.

Her husband, who was more worried about her welfare than he cared to admit, tactlessly gave her a blistering lecture on the evils of drink, worthy of a Methodist preacher. Kitty's remorse fled.

"You weren't exactly behaving like an angel yourself," she snapped. "Parading around the park with your mistress."

Lord Chesworth's thin face flushed with anger. "I told you that that affair is over. Mrs. Jackson asked me to escort her to the park where she was to meet a friend . . ."

"Hah!" said his wife nastily.

". . . to where, I repeat, she was to meet a friend."

"And where was the friend?"

"Oh, I don't know," shouted her husband, feeling guilty because he was sure that Veronica had invented the whole thing. "We didn't have time to look before you danced up, staggering and slobbering."

"I was not staggering or slobbering," screamed Kitty. "I was a bit tiddly, that's all. You still have not told me what you were doing in the park with that whore."

"I've told you," shouted her husband. "Don't try to put me in the wrong just because you're ashamed of having made a spectacle of yourself."

"Spectacle of myself? Spectacle of myself?" howled Kitty, jumping up and down.

"Stop repeating yourself like a bloody parrot. If you insist on behaving like a gutter-snipe, you'll be treated like one."

"Me behave like a guttersnipe? We were above your sort of behavior in Hampstead, my Lord."

"Nonsense. Utter twaddle! Your sort are hypocrites. Down on their knees in church on Sundays and straight into the house-maid's bed the rest of the week."

"My sort! What is my sort, you stupid lecher?"

Lord Chesworth had never been so angry. He looked straight at his infuriated wife and said, "Common."

The insult burned in the sudden silence between them.

Then Kitty's anger erupted again. Every humiliation she had suffered since she had married the Baron, burned before her eyes. Before he knew what she was about, she had picked up a vase of roses and dumped the contents over his head. "Why you little hellcat," he shouted. He grabbed hold of her arm and gave her a hearty smack on the backside and then howled with pain. Kitty was wearing her stays.

Kitty grabbed a handful of his black curls and banged his head against the wall. He gave her a tremendous push which sent her flying back onto the carpet and then dived on top of her, pinioning her hands above her head and staring down at her flushed, furious face.

The anger slowly died out of his eyes and was replaced by a mocking look. He grinned wickedly. "Now I've got you where I want you," he laughed and bent and kissed her.

Kitty kicked and struggled and tried to wrench her mouth away but he was lying on top of her and she found she could neither move nor fight the sensuous, languorous feeling that was seeping through her body. She gave a little groan and surrendered her mouth to his.

Suddenly, their attention was drawn to the door.

"Lady Henley and Mrs. Harrison," said the butler, staring straight ahead. Peter Chesworth raised his head and stared straight into the glittering eyes of Mrs. Harrison. The drawing room looked a wreck. Chairs and tables were overturned and Peter had roses caught in his hair and water dripping from his shoulders. Kitty, who was savagely wondering why *good* servants never knocked, tried to straighten her crumpled dress.

"How dare you!" said Mrs. Harrison.

"Now, now," said Lady Henley. "They're married, after all. We were passing and decided to give you a call. I'm feeling peckish, Kitty. Have you got anything to eat?"

The butler opened his mouth to say that dinner was to be served shortly, caught the look in his master's eyes, and closed his mouth again.

"We haven't got time to eat," said Mrs. Harrison. "I would like to know what business a detective from Scotland Yard has calling on me."

"There have been at least two attempts on your daughter's life," said Peter. "Surely we must do all we can to find out who is trying to kill her."

"It's all imagination," said Mrs. Harrison. "I've never heard such rubbish. You've all been reading too many novels. The detective was a most inferior vulgar person."

"She told him that too," said Lady Henley. Her stomach suddenly gave a protesting rumble and she looked down at it sadly like a mother looking down on an importunate child. "Well, if you ain't got any food, we'd better take ourselves off. Come on, Euphemia, we called at a bad time."

"We called just at the right time," said Mrs. Harrison, eyeing the disheveled pair.

"I hope things have not gone too far."

"Oh, come on," grumbled Lady Henley. "Anyone would think they weren't married the way you go on." Her stomach issued another huge rumble and she gave it a pat. Kitty tried not to giggle. Any minute now, she thought, she's going to say "there, there."

Mrs. Harrison backed from the room, still staring at them.

"Mrs. Veronica Jackson," the butler announced. Everyone froze and gazed at Veronica who sailed in. She looked radiantly lovely and her dress of her favorite scarlet emphasized the whiteness of her skin and the glossiness of her black hair.

Mrs. Harrison swept off, her back rigid with disapproval. Lady Henley lumbered after her, grumbling under her breath with her rumbling stomach adding a sort of counterpoint.

"I thought I would call and see how Kitty was," said Veronica brightly. Her blue eyes swept over the disordered pair and round the wreck of the room. "Been having a row?"

"Don't be impertinent," said Kitty. She rang the bell. "Mrs. Jackson is just leaving," she told the butler.

"This is the last time I pay a courtesy

call on you," snapped Veronica.

"Good," remarked Kitty indifferently, picking roses off the floor.

"Wait a minute, Veronica," said Peter. Here was a golden opportunity to explain matters to Veronica and get her out of his married life once and for all. Then he realized his mistake. Kitty gave him one shocked look and fled from the room.

The butler waited for a minute, looking from his master to Mrs. Jackson, and then left the room, closing the door quietly.

Peter ran his fingers through his hair. "This is one hell of a mess, Veronica. Look, I've got some explaining to do."

"I think you have," said Veronica with a slight smile.

She sat down gracefully on the sofa and patted the seat beside her. Peter sat down and took both her hands in his. He felt he must break it to her as gently as possible.

"We have had many happy times, Veronica," he began.

"Oh, yes, Peter," she sighed mistily.

"But the time has come when I must talk to you about my marriage. I —"

The butler reentered and Peter Chesworth swore. "There are several persons to see you, my Lord. They are creating a great disturbance. They say the name is Pugsley, my Lord."

"Oh, your wife's friends," said Veronica spitefully. "Send them in. You must see them, Peter." Veronica felt that Peter's resolve to rid himself of his wife would be strengthened by an introduction to Kitty's low acquaintances.

"You don't understand," said Peter desperately. But the butler was already announcing, "Mr. and Mrs. Pugsley and family."

The Pugsleys sidled in, gazing about them with their mouths open.

"Well, what is it?" demanded Peter.

"My Lord, my Lady," began Mrs. Pugsley and then stared at Veronica. " 'Ere, that's not our Kitty what you was 'olding 'ands with."

Mr. Pugsley grabbed his wife's arm and said in a stentorian whisper, "Shut yer gab. That's 'is fancy woman."

Veronica rose to her feet. "I must leave you with your fascinating friends, Peter darling." She kissed her fingers to him and sailed from the room, holding her little lace handkerchief pointedly to her nose as she passed the Pugsleys.

Mr. Pugsley took over as spokesman. "Now that 'er 'as gone," he said, "we'll come to the point. We've bin ruined, owing to that there fire what was caused by your good lady's party."

Lord Chesworth eyed him with distaste. "You want money, I suppose."

Bob Pugsley shuffled his feet. "Well, that's a bit crude-like, that way of puttin' it, but since you 'as put it — yes."

"I will need to consult my wife," said Peter icily. "Should she wish to give you anything more, I will suggest she sets up a trust for your children's care and education. Anything you want for yourself, Pugsley, I suggest you work for it."

"You got a job for me?" said Pugsley.

To his horror, his lordship smiled and said, "Yes, as a matter of fact I have. There is a cozy cottage available on my estate and the job of farm laborer that goes with it."

" 'Ere," said Bob Pugsley, grabbing his wife's arm for support. "Let's get out of 'ere."

"We ain't goin' nowheres, Bob Pugsley," said his wife, oblivious of the fact that her youngest was being sick on the carpet and that her eldest was trying to stuff a silver candlestick into his jacket. "We'll take it, my Lord, and gladly. And beggin' your pardon, I'm sure, I 'opes there ain't any 'ard liquor or dogs on your place."

Peter smiled and shook his head. He scribbled a note. "Here! That's to my agent. He'll start your husband working right away and help you set up the cottage."

Bob Pugsley saw the prison walls closing about him. "It's me back, me Lord," he yelled. He clutched his back, gave several artistic moans and fell to the carpet, calling faintly for brandy.

Mrs. Pugsley looked on unconcerned. "We're most grateful, your Lordship, ain't we Bob?" She pushed her moaning husband with her foot. "C'mon then, Bob, afore you dies of shock."

Showing surprising strength for such a small woman, she hauled her husband to his feet and marched him to the door. Her offspring fell into line behind her. "We'll pray for you, me Lord," said the eldest Pugsley child with an ingratiating smile.

"Thank you," said his lordship, putting his hand inside the child's jacket and recovering the candlestick. "Thank you very much."

When they had left, he gave a sigh of relief and went in search of his wife. She was in her bedroom, changing to go out.

"You need a maid," he remarked. "The

221

mysterious Colette seems to have disappeared along with the rest."

"I have done without a maid to dress me for most of my life, so I don't see why I need one now," said Kitty pettishly.

"Then you had better change your dressmaker," remarked her husband. "Who is going to fasten all those buttons on the back of that very pretty gown you're wearing?"

Kitty twisted around. In her agitation, she had left the back of her dress undone. "I'll do it myself," she said, fumbling behind her with the tiny buttons.

He watched her for a few seconds and then went to stand behind her. "Here, let me," he said quietly. "It's one of the things that husbands are good at."

"Particularly mine," said Kitty bitterly as his long fingers deftly fastened the buttons. "He's had *lots* of practice."

Peter took her by the shoulders and spun her around. "I've explained and explained to you about Mrs. Jackson. Don't you trust me?"

"No," said his wife, in a small voice.

He made an exasperated noise and bent to kiss her but she stayed motionless and unresponsive in his arms. He felt as if she had slapped him. He put her away from him and stormed to the door. "I'm going out."

"To Mrs. Jackson, I suppose," said Kitty, her large eyes bright with unshed tears.

"Damn Mrs. Jackson and damn you," raged her husband. "I'm going to my club — to get drunk."

He went out and slammed the door.

Kitty stared around the room, irresolute. If only she could trust him! She would take her problem to Emily Mainwaring.

Lady Mainwaring was at home working in her garden. She listened sympathetically to Kitty and then put down her gardening tools and came to sit at the table by the canal. "I believe him, you know," said Emily. "Veronica Jackson is a vulgar, grasping woman and your husband is too much of a gentleman to cope with that kind."

"I wondered if I could come back here and stay with you?" said Kitty.

Emily shook her head. "You know you have a home here any time you want but, my dear, at the moment I think you should be with your husband. Give him another chance. You can't keep running away. I'm sure he is very much in love with you."

Kitty looked at her with a cynicism that sat oddly on her young face. "Every time I trust him, Veronica pops up again."

Emily put her hand over Kitty's. "We're all invited to the Thackerays' place at Cowes. You didn't know? Probably Peter didn't have a chance to tell you.

"Now, you are surely sophisticated enough to cope with people like the Thackerays. Their jokes are a bit cruel but harmful only if you let yourself be hurt. They have a splendid yacht and it will make a very romantic setting for you and Peter. You're not going to let the Jackson woman just walk off with him, are you?"

Kitty shook her head.

"Good. I will travel down with you to ease any strain you may feel being alone with your husband."

Kitty smiled at the way Lady Mainwaring could discount a whole army of servants and consider that she would be "alone." But Lady Mainwaring, although she was a kind mistress, noticed her well-trained servants about as much as she did her furniture.

By evening, Kitty returned to her town house, feeling much calmer. At two in the morning, she heard her husband returning but he passed her bedroom en route to his own, without even pausing.

Chapter Eight

The Thackerays' house at Cowes was nautical to a fault: telescopes bristled at the windows; dinner was announced by a ship's bell instead of a gong; arriving guests were "piped aboard"; the Union Jack was hoisted up the flagpole in the garden every morning by Mr. Thackeray; and the water closet was referred to as "the head."

Looking more like Tweedledum and Tweedledee than ever, Mr. and Mrs. Thackeray were dressed in almost identical sailor suits except that hers had a skirt. The house was almost inevitably called "Davy Jones's Locker" and every liquid served in it from whiskey to tea was referred to as grog.

The Baron and Baroness were told to "walk about a bit and get their sea legs" which they interpreted to mean that they should retire to their rooms to change. It was with no little embarrassment that the pair discovered they had been allocated the same bedroom. Kitty eyed the large double bed as if it were some peculiar instrument of torture. While her husband went to remove a large pair of lobsters from the foot of it and send them off to their rightful place in the kitchens, Kitty looked out of the window.

The sun sparkled on the Solent and Peter, moving to his wife's side, pointed out King Edward's yacht, the *Victoria and Albert*, tacking across the blue water. The couple had been able to chat easily on the train, encouraged by Emily Mainwaring who had kept up a steady flow of light conversation to cover any awkward moments of silence.

"We're going sailing on the Thackerays' schooner this afternoon, if you feel up to it," said Peter. "But do remember to go to the . . . well . . . water closet before you leave. The Royal Yacht Club doesn't have any facilities for ladies. Trousers are definitely forbidden so you will need to wear a skirt."

Kitty began to feel happy again. "I'm very excited, Peter," she exclaimed. "I've never been on a yacht be—"

She broke off and stared down into the driveway, her face turning white and tense. Being helped down from a carriage by the "Bishop of Zanzibar" was Veronica Jackson. All Kitty's miserable memories of her previous visit to the Thackerays came back and she burst into tears.

Peter drew her over to the bed and sat down beside her. He took her hands away gently, from her face. "Kitty, I've told you I love you and I mean it. Veronica means nothing to me."

"She's here, isn't she?" sobbed Kitty. "And she's got that terrible young man with her."

"Who, Cyril Lawton? He's a bit of a silly chump, that's all."

Kitty told her husband for the first time about Cyril's impersonation of the "Bishop" and her confession. Peter groaned and gathered her closer. "I'm a beast. I never thought that picture meant so much to you. I must have been drunk out of my skull. Kitty, we're going to stick very close together on this visit. Do you hear me? No one is going to play nasty practical jokes on you and no one is going to try to murder you, and Veronica Jackson is *not* going to come between us."

She looked up at him anxiously, hoping to believe him. He hugged her close. "Just trust me, Kitty. Dry your eyes. That's my girl. Now give me a kiss."

She raised her tear-stained face to his, smiling tremulously. As he bent his head, there was a loud banging at the door. "Hurry up in there. All aboard that's going aboard!"

They got to their feet and looked at each other. Peter gave her a quick kiss. "We'd better go. Let's get changed quickly." He started to throw off his clothes until he caught his wife's anxious look and retreated to the privacy of the bathroom. With a feeling of dressing for a masquerade, Kitty put on a white sailor jacket and white shirt. By the time she had perched a jaunty sailor hat on her head, her husband was ready.

They met Cyril Lawton, the "Bishop," at the top of the stairs. "Cyril, my dear, dear chap," said the Baron, grasping Cyril's arm in a warm grip. "Do step along to my room for a minute so I can have a word with you. Go on downstairs and wait for me, Kitty." The protesting Cyril was dragged off along the corridor.

Veronica Jackson was waiting with the rest of the party and Kitty noticed, with a sinking heart, that Veronica was wearing exactly the same outfit.

"Really, I must fire that dressmaker of mine," announced Veronica. "She seems to be handing out her toiles to every little nobody."

"Obviously," said Kitty sweetly. "Since she gave one to you."

Before Veronica could reply, Peter Chesworth arrived with Cyril in tow. Cyril had a huge purple bruise forming under his right eye and explained to the anxious guests that he had tripped and fallen against the bedpost. Ignoring Veronica, Peter walked forward and put an arm around his wife's waist. He gave her a slight hug and in reply to the unspoken question in her eyes, gave her a mocking wink. Kitty burst out laughing; she knew how Cyril had received his bruise. The couple walked out into the sunshine and Veronica's eyes bored into their backs.

Once they were aboard the Thackerays' schooner, Kitty sank back against the cushions in the bow with her husband's arm around her and gave a sigh of pure pleasure. Nothing else seemed real except the presence of her husband, and Veronica buzzed away on the corner of her vision like an angry wasp.

"Your mama and Lady Henley are coming to join us this evening," said Peter lazily, as the schooner cut across the blue waters of the Solent like an arrow, with the crew doing all the work and Mr. Thackeray running around taking all the credit.

"What does Lady Henley do when the Thackerays play practical jokes?" asked Kitty.

"She doesn't even notice them," said her husband. "Last summer she was here and they did the bladder-under-the-plate trick of theirs at dinner. She kept on eating regardless, chasing her plate all over the table like a foxhound hot on the scent. Then she simply picked up the plate and ate from her lap."

Kitty laughed and her husband kissed her cheek. "I'm just going off to have a word with Thackeray. He knows some chap who's selling off farm machinery, cheap. You'll be all right, won't you?"

"What on earth could happen to me here?" Kitty laughed. "Off you go."

Oblivious of the curious stares of the rest of the guests, he kissed his wife — a thoroughly unfashionable piece of behavior — and went off whistling.

Veronica Jackson thought at that moment that she would die from hate. So she was to be cast off in favor of this young girl in the very way her husband had abandoned her for the American heiress. Well, Peter Chesworth was not going to have his cake and eat it. Through eyes dimmed with fury, Veronica saw Kitty's slim figure

230

standing by the rail. She took a quick look around. No one was looking.

Kitty was watching the water sparkling in the wake of the schooner. She was absolutely and completely happy. "I shall remember this moment until the day I die," she thought — and then screamed. A ferocious shove sent her flying over the rail and into the icy water. She flailed her arms and choked and screamed again, seeing the schooner disappearing rapidly like a toy boat in the distance, then there was a roaring in her ears and she began to sink.

"I will not die, I will not die!" she thought fiercely. She thrashed her arms blindly and for one blessed moment took a gulp of sweet, fresh air and saw the white and scarlet of a cork lifebuoy floating a few yards away.

Kitty could not swim but, summoning all her strength and trying to push the blind panic from her mind, she flailed her arms in front of her, trying to copy the motions of the swimmers she had seen in the Serpentine. Inch by inch she drew closer and, just when she felt she would die from sheer exhaustion as she thrashed about in her water-logged clothes, the lifebuoy was suddenly against her face and she put her arms tightly around it and held on for dear life.

Then the schooner seemed to reappear suddenly and hove to and a small boat put out from it. One minute she was gasping and struggling in the water and the next, it seemed, she was lying in her husband's arms in the dingy. Kitty gave him one scared look and fainted.

Veronica Jackson's attempt on Kitty's life had been seen by Mrs. Thackeray who had sounded the alarm. Kicking, biting, screaming, and appealing to Peter for help, Veronica had been locked in the cabin while Mr. Thackeray ran from side to side of his vessel, letting off every lifebuoy on the schooner and sending them bobbing back across the water in the direction of Kitty. Peter Chesworth set out in the dingy, cursing the oarsmen to greater efforts, his eyes watering with the strain of trying to spot his wife in the glittering water.

At last he saw her, clinging to the lifebuoy on the crest of a wave, and he sent up a silent prayer of thanks. When she was hauled aboard, he clutched her to him and swore to himself that he would get her to the safety of Reamington Hall as soon as possible and never let her out of his sight again.

★ ★ ★

The silent party made their way ashore and across the lawns of the Royal Yacht Club. Scandal must be avoided at all costs. Imprisoned between two burly members of the crew, Veronica was hustled into a closed carriage. She was to be locked in her room until it was decided what to do with her. Kitty, who had recovered consciousness, was also hustled to her room to await the doctor. She was feeling absolutely exhausted and waived the sedative that the doctor tried to give her.

Peter Chesworth looked in on his sleeping wife and then went downstairs to where the much-flustered Thackerays told him in unison that there was a detective from Scotland Yard waiting for him in the study.

Then they both stood amazed as the Baron merely said, "Thank God," and went into the study and closed the door on their astonished faces.

Mr. Albert Grange got to his feet. "It seems as if I've arrived at the right moment, my Lord, but I'm very surprised to learn the identity of the lady."

Peter Chesworth sat down heavily and sighed. "I find it hard to believe myself," he said. "It doesn't explain the peculiar behavior of the servants at our town house.

In fact, apart from the last attempt, none of the previous ones seem to fit in with what I know of Mrs. Jackson's character. Although, I'm beginning to wonder if I know her at all. I don't want to press charges and make a lot of unnecessary scandal but I want to make sure that my wife is going to be safe." Peter Chesworth shook his head. "Perhaps after you have a word with Mrs. Jackson, we can decide on the best course of action."

"I would like to try something if I may, my Lord," said Mr. Grange. "I would like to gather everyone together who has been close to your wife, namely, yourself, Lady Mainwaring, Lady Henley, Mrs. Harrison, and, of course, Mrs. Jackson."

"Very well," said the Baron ringing the bell.

One by one, the ladies assembled in the study, eyeing the little detective nervously. Veronica Jackson looked completely crumpled, all her flamboyance gone.

"Now then, ladies and my Lord," began the detective, and then paused as he heard a timid knock at the door. He opened it and Kitty stood on the threshold.

"My dear," said Peter crossing to her side, "I'm sure this is all going to be too much for you."

"Let her stay," said Mr. Grange. "If her Ladyship shows signs of being unwell, we can ring for help."

Mr. Grange produced his notebook. "Now then, Mrs. Jackson. You tried to kill Baroness Reamington this afternoon. But there were previous attempts on her life." He listed the snakes, the broken balcony, and the attempt at Sloane Square underground station.

Veronica stared at him in horror. "I had nothing to do with it," she screamed. "Yes, I pushed her off the yacht because — because — *you* wanted her dead, Peter."

"What rubbish is this?" snapped the Baron.

"But you did," wailed Veronica, now thoroughly terrified. "You came to me on her wedding night. You spent it with me. You said if she were dead you would have all her money and be able to marry me. Me!" She stabbed a finger at her bosom and looked wildly around the room.

Kitty stumbled to her feet and made blind groping motions toward the door.

"Kitty!" pleaded her husband. He held her arm and she stared down at his hand and then collapsed to the floor in a dead faint.

"This is ridiculous!" expostulated Peter.

"My wife is at the end of her tether. I'll just carry her to her room."

The detective rang the bell. "Sit down, my Lord." There was a note of steel in his voice and his eyes held Peter's. He waited until the butler had arranged for Kitty to be carried back to her room and then addressed the group.

"I will see Mrs. Jackson and Lord Chesworth alone," said the detective, holding the door open for the others.

Mrs. Harrison suddenly sprang to life, "Murderer!" she screamed and flung herself on Peter Chesworth and tried to rake his face with her nails. With surprising strength, Lady Henley pulled her off. Mrs. Harrison burst into noisy tears and was led from the room.

"Now, my Lord," said Mr. Grange in a grim voice. He signaled to a policeman by the door who took out his notebook.

"Oh, put that away just now," said Peter wearily. "This is going to be hard enough for me to talk about without that great oaf writing down every word I say."

"All right, then," said the detective. "Begin at the beginning."

And Peter Chesworth did, leaving nothing out, while Veronica Jackson sat as if turned to stone. Everyone — the detective, the policeman, and Veronica — were aware that they were hearing an honest confession of a man's growing love for his wife.

"I have no alibi for Hadsea because obviously someone was hired to saw through the balcony," said Peter. "But I have a definite alibi for the time she was at the underground station."

"Someone could have been hired on that occasion as well," said the detective. "But I'll tell you something, my Lord. I believe you and this lady here. But someone is trying to kill your wife. For the moment, Mrs. Jackson has made one attempt and it's up to your wife whether she wishes to press charges or not.

"In any case, I am taking you both back to London with me. I want whoever it is to be convinced that you both have been found guilty."

"What good will that do?" said Peter. "And who will be here to protect her? You're taking me away and leaving my wife with her murderer."

"Exactly, my Lord. Your wife will be well guarded at all times. I will have two good plainclothesmen introduced into the staff here and they will watch every step she takes. This is the one way we will get the murderer to show himself — or herself."

Emily Mainwaring found Kitty standing by the window of her bedroom watching the party leaving for London in the driveway below. In the light of the carriage lamps, her husband's white face looked up toward her bedroom. She turned from the window and flung herself on the bed, dying as if her heart would break.

"He didn't do it. I just know he didn't do it," said Emily Mainwaring over and over again, patting Kitty in an ineffectual way on the shoulder.

"It doesn't matter what he's done," sobbed Kitty. "He's with *her*. They planned it all between them. She said so. And you should have seen the look on Peter's face."

"Nonsense!" said Emily stoutly. "I just *know* it was Veronica all along. But you're safe now, anyway. Are you going to press charges?"

"Yes — no. Oh, I don't know. I wish I were dead," wailed Kitty. "I don't want to stay here with all these — all these — *tickey* people."

"You shall no more," said a voice from the doorway. It was Ladly Henley, a massive shadow in the darkening room. She lumbered forward. "Your mama asked me to get you out of this. I've a little place along the coast. You can potter about a bit and get your nerves in order and Emily can tell your husband where to find you . . . if you think that's wise."

Kitty thought of all the people downstairs, the Thackeryas with their silly iokes, Cyril Lawton who had heard her "confession," and the rest of the guests all knowing that her husband had been having an affair with Veronica Jackson. Still she hesitated.

"I also thought you ought to know, Henry Dwight-Hammond has just driven up in that motorcar of his," said Lady Henley.

That clinched it. "I'll go," said Kitty wearily. "But don't tell my husband. I need time to think."

Mr. Albert Grange was thinking much the same thing as he turned the key in the door of his cozy home in Fulham. He needed time to think.

Veronica Jackson had been warned not to leave town and a policeman had been stationed outside her house. The same applied to Lord Chesworth. Albert Grange kissed his wife and followed her into the bright kitchen with a frown on his face. His wife, Amy, sighed. For the hundredth time, she wished her husband had a normal job like some of the other neighbors' husbands. For years Albert had been telling her that he would take their savings out of the bank and buy a snug little pub in the country, but there always seemed to be one more case that he must solve — and then one more. So for the hundredth time, she laid the table, poured her husband a glass of beer, and said, "Why don't you talk about it, love?"

Albert sipped his beer and began with a weary sigh, to outline the case to his wife. "On the face of it," he said, after he had finished his summary, "it should be a conspiracy between my lord and Mrs. Jackson. But I swear the man is honestly in love with his wife. On the other hand, I'm sure it's one of these here creem passionellies."

His wife kissed him on the nose. "Now then, Albert Grange, I think you're getting carried away by love in high society. You always were one for telling me that once you got out of the working classes, money was the biggest motive."

"Well, that's true for sure," said Albert. "But Lord Chesworth got his wife's money by way of a marriage settlement and she, Lady Chesworth, don't get the bulk of her mama's fortune until Mrs. Harrison dies."

Amy Grange rattled the dishes thoughtfully. "But you say Mrs. Harrison's not in good health and someone is trying to kill her daughter. So who gets the money then? They haven't any children."

Albert Grange looked at her with a startled expression. "Now why didn't I think of that. Although the old girl looks so crazy these days, she might have left the whole lot to a home for aging cats."

"Now eat your supper and forget about the whole thing until tomorrow," said his wife.

Albert rubbed his thinning hair so that the oiled strands stood up in spikes. "I can't, Amy. I better run down to the Yard and get a message to Cowes. I've got to find out the name of Mrs. Harrison's solicitor." And he rushed out of the kitchen, leaving his wife to look at another ruined meal.

It was late by the time Mr. Grange left the Yard. But the little detective did not go home. Instead, he walked along the Embankment, his head sunk in his collar. The participants in the case danced through his head like the lights on the water. He would just call on Lord Chesworth. For some reason he trusted that young man.

His lordship was in the library, sunk in melancholy, reflecting on his disastrous marriage and worried to death about his wife. He practically dragged the little detective into the room. "Any news of my wife?"

"Her ladyship is all right as far as we know," said Mr. Grange. "But my good wife has just come up with a bit of an idea." He outlined Amy's suggestion about the will. "Like I see it, my Lord, I don't know as I should be talking to you like this. If the money goes to you, then you're in trouble."

"I can set your mind at ease," said Peter. "Mrs. Harrison hates me. She would never leave me a penny."

"Maybe your Lordship would like to accompany me to the solicitor tomorrow. We should have his name by then."

"Of course," said Peter. "I only wish we didn't have to wait until then. It's going to be a long night."

Albert Grange groaned. "Give me a good old knifing in the Mile End Road any day, my Lord. These high-society crimes are a pain in the neck. I've got the Commissioner breathing down my neck every step of the way. 'Got to handle these people with kid gloves,' he says. Pah! Murder is murder whether it's in Limehouse or Mayfair."

After the detective had left, Peter Chesworth sat looking out at the dark, London sky. What if Mrs. Harrison hadn't made a will? Then they would be back where they started. Unless the murderer were found, his marriage was finished. He picked up a book and prepared to sit out the night.

It was after nine o'clock the following morning before the little detective appeared. "I've got it," he said bursting into the library without ceremony. "Her solicitors are Fordyce, Fordyce & Bramble of Cheapside. Grab your hat and coat, my Lord, and let's go."

Peter Chesworth called for his carriage and the two men sat tense and silent on the road to the city. What a lot of confounded traffic there was, thought Peter Chesworth savagely. Fleet Street seemed to be jammed from the Temple to Ludgate Circus with buses and hansoms and four-wheelers. If he ever got out of this mess he would buy a motor car and to hell with tradition!

But at last they reached Cheapside. Mr. James Fordyce himself would see them. Peter Chesworth realized why the astute detective had brought him along. Mr.

243

Fordyce was inclined to hem and haw about disclosing the contents of his client's will to a "person" from Scotland Yard. Peter Chesworth realized with some surprise what a lot of social snubs people like Albert Grange had to put up with. But the little detective ignored it and, said, "I'm sure Lord Chesworth — you know Baron Reamington, I'm sure — will support me when I say that it is a matter of life and death."

An oily smile creased the lawyer's unlovely features. "I did not realize we had such distinguished company, my Lord. But of course if you say it is all right, my Lord, then, my Lord, I see no reason to hesitate."

He rang a bell on his desk and told the clerk to bring the Harrison papers. "What an unconscionable time the old fool was taking coming to the point," thought Peter savagely. The lawyer hemmed and hawed and "yes — yessed" for what seemed an age and then he suddenly looked up.

Ignoring the detective he said, "What it amounts to, my Lord, is that all Mrs. Harrison's fortune goes to her daughter in the event of her death. If her daughter should die childless, then the whole estate goes to . . . Lady Amelia Henley."

He stared in surprise as the two men sat

as if turned to stone. "Yes, yes," he said fussily. "It's all here . . . 'to my dear friend and companion, Lady Henley.' "

The detective and Lord Chesworth got to their feet as if rising from a dream. Then Mr. Grange sprang into action. "The railroad station, my Lord, quick!"

They caught the train just as it was moving out. Peter sank back in the carriage and stared at his companion. "But that fat old glutton. It's incredible!"

But Mr. Grange felt on his home ground. The bizarre case had taken on a comfortable everyday appearance.

"I was a bit confused because of all the society people involved, my Lord, but when you get down to it, this sort of murder happens all over London. Greed for money knows no social barriers, my Lord."

His lordship suddenly smiled at the little detective. "Since we're going to be spending a bit of time together, you may as well call me 'Peter.' "

Mr. Grange scratched his head under his bowler hat in perplexity. "Well, it'll seem a bit strange and forward-like but well — here goes, Peter."

"That's the ticket, Albert," said Peter, dazzling the detective with his most charming smile and picking up his news-paper.

Albert Grange sat sucking on his empty pipe and staring into space. A lifetime of social snubs melted before his eyes. "Peter." Just wait till he told Amy.

Lord Chesworth tried to concentrate on the headlines of the *Daily Telegraph* but they seemed to dance before his eyes. He put down the paper with a groan.

"Pray to God we're in time, Albert. Just pray to God we're in time."

Chapter Nine

Lady Henley sat up in her bed at the Thackerays' Cowes home and watched her maid, Jenkins, packing the trunks.

"Can't you move any faster, girl?" she snapped.

"I'm doing that best I can, my Lady," said Jenkins sulkily.

Lady Henley stuffed another slab of toast into her capacious mouth. "I don't know what servants are coming to these days," she said grumpily.

"Nor I, my Lady," said Jenkins, eager to impart gossip and turn attention from herself. "They've got two new footmen downstairs and you never saw the like."

Lady Henley put down her cup and surveyed her maid with interest. "Something strange about them?"

"Oh, definitely, my Lady. They don't do any work and just lounge about the place asking questions. The butler wanted them fired on the spot but Mr. Thackeray, he says to leave them alone."

The bedclothes started to fly in all directions as the huge mass that was Lady Henley heaved herself out onto the floor.

"Get me dressed immediately, girl. And then finish that packing in double-time. And if you can't do it fast enough, get one of the housemaids to help you."

Jenkins began to dress her mistress, wondering if she would ever get over the feeling of distaste that this part of her job caused her. First the huge corsets which must have taken every bone out of a whole whale had to be fitted on and the sagging fat pushed into place. Then the lacing which strained every muscle. Then the silk stockings had to be strained onto the massive legs and the suspenders stretched down over the bulging thighs to meet them. And then at last the enormous drawers of crepe de chine and the worst was over, bar the arranging of Lady Henley's hank of thin, greasy hair.

Jenkins dreamt of finding a job with a slim, young, fashionable mistress but she knew it was impossible. She had done time in Holloway Prison for theft and Lady Henley had found her through some charitable organization which helped women prisoners to find work on the outside. In return for this, Jenkins had to suffer being treated like a dog for a yearly pittance. But at least she was housed and fed, particularly well fed, since Lady Henley spent all her money on food.

Having decided at last that her hairstyle was satisfactory, Lady Henley crammed an enormous crimson toque down on it and waddled from the room.

She found Kitty in her bedroom arranging her own packing and sobbing over a cravat of her husband's.

"Now, my dear," said Lady Henley, "you must pull yourself together for your husband's sake. I'm sure he is innocent. Let me ring for a couple of girls to do this packing and we'll be on our way." She rang the bell and bustled about with surprising energy.

Kitty was too numb with misery to take any part in the proceedings. In no time at all, she was hustled out of the house and into the carriage which was directed to the railroad station.

"I thought we were just going along the coast," said Kitty in surprise, surfacing briefly from her despair.

"And so we are," said her large companion. "I'll tell you why we're going this way when we get on the train. Leave the baggage in the carriage."

Kitty complied and Jenkins looked at her

mistress thoughtfully. She had been witness to an interesting scene in the kitchen before she left. The butler, harassed by complaints about the new footmen from the other servants, had finally called them all together and confided that the two new servants were in fact gentlemen from Scotland Yard who were employed to guard the Baroness. Jenkins had noticed the two gentlemen in question following them in another carriage at a discreet distance, and felt oddly reassured.

To Jenkins's surprise, Lady Henley bought three first-class tickets for London and insisted that she accompany them instead of traveling third class as usual.

As the train started to move out of the station, Lady Henley turned to Kitty.

"Now, my dear, I don't want to frighten you more than need be, but why we are traveling this way is because I noticed two very rough characters following us."

Jenkins opened her mouth to explain about the plainclothesmen and closed it again as she received a vicious, warning look from Lady Henley.

"So, my dear," her ladyship went on, laying a pudgy hand on Kitty's knee, "just to be on the safe side, I've thought of a little ruse. I've sent the carriage with the luggage on to the next station to wait for us. We'll wait till the train is just pulling out and then jump out — not onto the platform but onto the tracks on the other side of the train."

Kitty was too tired after her sleepless night and too frightened to do more than nod. All she wanted to do was get away somewhere safe with the reassuring figure of Lady Henley and to have time to think.

Jenkins looked at her mistress in puzzled alarm. She began to feel uneasy. There could only be one explanation of why Lady Henley wanted to avoid the men from Scotland Yard. But then perhaps Lady Henley did not know they were from Scotland Yard.

The train chugged into a quiet country station and the three woman waited anxiously in the corridor. At the sound of the guard's whistle, Lady Henley said, "Now!" and opening the corridor door, nipped down onto the tracks with surprising agility.

In the next compartment on the train one of the plainclothesmen drew his head in as the train started to move. "No one got off here," he said to his companion. "Waste of time, this, if you ask me. I'm sure the husband's the one who's behind all them murder attempts. Him and that fancy woman of his."

His companion nodded in agreement. "At least the Baroness is all right with Lady Henley. Now, Lady Henley — she's top-drawer — not like that there Mrs. Jackson."

Both settled back comfortably, enjoying the rare luxury of a first-class compartment, and the train steamed off.

The three women picked their way in silence across the tracks. The little station was deserted. With Jenkins pushing from the back and Kitty pulling from the front, they managed to heave Lady Henley's bulk onto the platform.

They made their way to the carriage and with a crack of the coachman's whip, they traveled down to the coast and started to follow the road along the shore. The day was in keeping with Kitty's low spirits. Both sky and sea were a uniform gray. There wasn't a breath of wind and they seemed to be the only moving thing in the landscape for miles.

Then the carriage suddenly swung off from the main road and bumped along a country lane that was bordered on either side by huge thorn hedges.

"This house has been in my family for a long time although I hardly ever use it," said Lady Henley, breaking a long silence. "It's a little neglected but I'm sure you won't mind, Kitty. All you need is a bit of a holiday with your old friend."

Kitty gave her a weak smile. "Please don't think I'm taking all this for granted, Lady Henley. It's just that I'm so upset. . . ."

"I know, I know," said Lady Henley soothingly. "We're nearly there."

The carriage turned and twisted up a rutted driveway, hedged in by uncut bushes and tangled undergrowth. Suddenly, they rattled into an open clearing. "Well, there it is," said Lady Henley. "It's called Pevvy Chase, though that's a pretty grand name for such a poky place."

The house was a redbrick Georgian gem with a shell-shaped fanlight over its pillared door. The door was opened by a thin, scrawny housekeeper and Jenkins stiffened like a cat, suddenly aware of danger. She knew that kind of woman better than anyone. Prison left its mark on the hands and eyes. Well, she supposed Lady Henley must be in the habit of recruiting ex-prisoners and paying them cheap. Who was she — poor Jenkins — to get so up-pity?

Kitty exclaimed in delight at the charming hallway with its delicately molded doors. The housekeeper led the way up a slim-balustered staircase lit by an oval window, to the bedrooms above. "Here you are, my Lady," she said, throwing open the door and bobbing an awkward curtsy. "You get a fine view of the water."

Running to the window and looking out, Kitty saw with surprise that they were again at the seaside. The road had twisted and turned so much, hidden by its high hedges, that she had assumed they must be well inland. But the uncut lawn sloped down to a small terraced garden with red-brick steps, that led to a small beach hedged on either side by woods growing right down to the water's edge.

She jumped as she heard Lady Henley's voice in her ear. "You can go for long ram-bles, my dear," said her ladyship. "Get the color back in your cheeks. Now, I know you're tired and have been a long time on the road and so I think we should have an early dinner and then retire. Jenkins will help you dress since you haven't a maid of your own. Remember, Jenkins, no chattering." She wagged a plump finger playfully at the maid who, to Kitty's surprise, cringed as if Lady Henley had waved her fist.

After Lady Henley left, Jenkins deftly set about getting Kitty dressed for dinner. Kitty was pleased and surprised at her calm, impersonal efficiency. She had only known the cold, insolent touch of Colette's fingers when it came to being attended to by a maid.

She sat down at the dressing table and let Jenkins arrange her hair. "You don't need to use these pads, my Lady," said Jenkins. "You've got plenty of lovely hair. See, I'll just arrange it in a simple style. It will look just as good and feel ever so much more comfortable."

Kitty smiled up at the maid. "I think you're a treasure, Jenkins. I feel like stealing you away from Lady Henley."

"I wish you could," said Jenkins bitterly, and then bit her lip. "I'm sorry, my Lady, I didn't mean to say that. You won't tell her Ladyship on me, will you?"

"No, of course not," said Kitty surprised at the girl's fear. Jenkins gave a correct curtsy and left the room.

How odd, thought Kitty. As if anyone could be afraid of Lady Henley! There was no gas or electricity in the old house but plenty of candles and oil lamps. Feeling as if she were living in the eighteenth century, Kitty picked up a candle and made her way downstairs to the dining room.

During the meal, Kitty began to wonder if living in close proximity to Lady Henley's gluttony was going to be bearable. Her Ladyship had abandoned her massive stays along with any of the restraints of good social behavior and ate . . . well . . . like a pig, thought Kitty. She chomped, she slobbered, she gulped, her eyes taking on a glazed look as the dessert was served.

Lady Henley obviously kept a very good cook. The dessert was wild strawberries soaked in kirsch topped with whipped cream and served in wafer-thin meringue shells. But Kitty dropped her fork after the first mouthful. The sight of her hostess was enough to turn anyone's stomach. Instead of using her fork, Lady Henley was cramming the meringue confections into her mouth whole. Meringue powder floated around her like incense around the body of an obese buddha.

Then came the savory of grilled bacon and oysters on toast. At least she can't make much mess with that, thought Kitty, and gave a sigh of relief when dinner came to an end. Picking her teeth with a goose quill, Lady Henley eyed her guest. "You know something, Kitty? I'll tell you something, I ain't told anyone else. I eat too much."

Kitty smiled faintly. After the exhibition at dinner, how was she supposed to reply?

"So-o-o," said her hostess, impaling a sliver of food on her toothpick and looking at it with interest, "I've decided to do some walking. Don't want to die before me time, heh!"

She gave a Falstaffian laugh which sent the candle flames dancing and the shadows of her great bulk running around the room. Kitty wondered why people considered candlelight romantic. Why, it made the genial Lady Henley look positively sinister.

"Anyway," went on Lady Henley, "why don't you go for a walk in the woods tomorrow and explore. You won't get lost. There's a huge tree out in front of the house that's been blasted by lightning. You can see it sticking up for miles."

Kitty said that she had planned to spend the morning writing letters.

"Worst thing you could do," said Lady Henley. "It'll start you brooding. No — exercise is the thing."

By morning when the sun was once again sparkling on the sea and the birds singing in the woods, Kitty decided it would be a good idea to go exploring after all. Lady Henley walked out to the entrance steps with her. "Go that way," she said, waving a piece of buttered toast in the direction of the east. "Supposed to be some sort of old Roman fort there."

Kitty set off into the woods with a feeling of relief at leaving her hostess behind. She could not understand her burning desire to put as much distance between herself and the house as possible, but she walked on into the thicker part of the woods, occasionally stopping to untangle her skirt from a briar or to watch the squirrels foraging for food in the undergrowth. The trees grew taller and thicker and the woods became quieter. Nothing seemed to stir except the topmost branches of the trees rustling and sighing as they were swept by the wind from the sea. Turning over the puzzle of her husband and Veronica Jackson, wondering who to believe, Kitty suddenly became aware of her surroundings and realized that she was tired and hungry and that the sun was high overhead, meaning that it must be around noon.

She looked up for a sign of the blasted tree that Lady Henley had mentioned but the trees in this part of the woods were too tall. With the beginnings of a feeling of unease, she started to make her way back. After walking for what seemed miles, her stockings torn by briars, and a blister beginning to form on her heel, Kitty found herself among some smaller trees and looking across, she could see the top of the blasted tree on the horizon. With a sigh of relief, she began to make her way toward it.

After several miles more, she sat down and nearly cried with panic and exhaustion. The sun was beginning to slide down the sky and the shadows of the woods were lengthening. Although she tried to keep her eyes on it, the dead tree that was her landmark seemed to move and shift, dancing among the other trees from west to southwest as if it were enchanted. Kitty sat very still and listened to see if she could hear any sounds of human life to guide her. Then she heard it. Away to her left came the faint slurring sound of the sea. She plunged back into the undergrowth and followed the sound. In a surprisingly short time, she found herself peering through a mass of dead shrubbery at the sea. Taking off her boots, she gingerly stepped into the water which came up to her knees and started to wade back along the shore. Dusk had fallen by the time she edged around the last of the trees and found herself on the little beach at Pevvy Chase. Figures came running down the lawn to meet her and she could distinguish her hostess's vast bulk in the gathering gloom.

"We've been searching all day for you," gasped Lady Henley. "This is our local magistrate, Sir Henry Gibbons. He's had his men combing the woods all afternoon."

Lady Henley led her into the hall and she found herself being addressed by the tall, thin figure of the magistrate. "You really should not wander around these woods by yourself," said Sir Henry reprovingly. "Anyone from these parts will tell you that it's uncommonly easy to lose your way."

To Kitty's surprise, she heard Lady Henley agreeing. "Just what I told her myself," said her hostess with a bland smile. "But these young gels will wander off on their own."

Kitty was too tired to argue. She allowed

Jenkins to lead her off to her room and change her torn and soiled clothes. The maid seemed unusually nervous and kept glancing at the door. Finally Jenkins said in a whisper, "If you was to know of a girl what had a bad background but was reformed-like and a very good maid, would you take her on, my Lady?"

Kitty looked at her in surprise. "I'm sure I would take on anyone you could recommend. Did she do something bad?"

"Well, my Lady," said Jenkins, still looking anxiously at the door and pleating her apron between her trembling fingers, "this here girl come from a terribly poor family, my Lady. She fell in love with this young man. A clerk he was, a bit above her in station. Well one day this young man asks her to go walking with him, but she had nothing to wear that you would call anywheres nice.

"So this girl, my Lady, saw this real pretty shawl in a shop, just a-lying on the counter where a customer who had been looking at it had left it. Well, she thought as how lovely it would look and how it would cover her shabby old dress and 'fore you know what had happened, she'd stuffed it into her reticule and hopped it out onto the street. She was caught a few yards from the shop door, tried, and sent to Holloway Prison."

Kitty's senses seemed suddenly sharpened by fatigue. "You're talking about yourself, aren't you Jenkins?" she said gently.

The maid burst into tears. "Oh yes, my Lady. Please get me away from Lady Henley or she'll do us both harm."

"Oh, come, come," said Kitty. "Lady Henley has gone out of her way to take care of me."

Jenkins bent her head close to Kitty's. "How come then she sent you off into them woods? I heard her. How come she got you away from them two men on the train? 'Cause they was Scotland Yard men, that's why. How come —"

She broke off with her hands to her mouth as Lady Henley entered.

"If you're finished here, Jenkins," snapped Lady Henley, "get about your duties."

Jenkins scurried out with her head bowed. "Has she been gossipping?" asked Lady Henley.

Kitty shook her head. "She never said a word," she lied. Her hostess gave a fat smile. "Feel up to a bit of dinner?"

Kitty refused and said she would settle

for a tray in her room and bade her large hostess a firm good night.

She was finally left alone with the beginnings of terror. She must try to speak some more to Jenkins. But Lady Henley could not be trying to harm her. It had been Veronica Jackson all along. And with a bitter stab of jealousy, Kitty did so want it to be Veronica Jackson. Why, Lady Henley had hardly enough energy to move across the room!

But she was to change her mind on the following morning, when Lady Henley arrived at the breakfast table in tweeds and strong boots and announced that they were going for a walk. Kitty protested that she was still too tired after her adventure of the day before. "Nonsense," said Lady Henley. "I need my exercise and after all I've done for you, Kitty, I don't think it's too much to ask you to help me take my exercise." She pouted like some grotesque baby and Kitty felt obliged to humor her.

The day was overcast and windy. Great, ragged clouds flew across the stormy black surface of the sea and the trees around the old house waved their arms and let out a loud groaning sigh as the ill-assorted pair walked off down the driveway.

Kitty began to feel reassured. Lady Henley kept up an amusing flow of conversation of what society was like in Victorian times. She seemed so jolly and normal that Kitty decided the only thing sinister about Lady Henley was her appetite. She chatted amiably, trying to keep worried thoughts about her husband at the back of her mind, unaware that Peter Chesworth was scouring the countryside looking for her.

The two plainclothesmen had been given a tongue-lashing by the furious Albert Grange and then every station between Cowes and London had been painstakingly searched. No one had noticed three women alighting from the train. They seemed to have disappeared into thin air.

Kitty was strictly a town girl but even her inexperienced eyes noticed that the surrounding countryside was badly in need of cultivation. Some of the tangled hedges practically met above their heads and they seemed to walk further and further away from the house down endless tunnels of green gloom.

At last Lady Henley broke through a gap in the hedge and led Kitty across an uncultivated stretch of field toward a farm worker's cottage at the far end. "One of the tenants," she explained. "We'll call in and have a bite of luncheon."

Kitty agreed with relief, looking forward to sitting down and resting her aching feet.

Lady Henley rapped smartly on the door with her walking stick. There was a sound of slow steps within and then the door opened.

With an evil smile creasing his white slab of a face, stood Kitty's ex-butler, Checkers.

Kitty half turned to run when a smacking blow from Lady Henley's walking stick struck her on the side of the head and she fell unconscious.

When she regained consciousness she was tied firmly to a chair with her hands behind her back. On the other side of the kitchen table sat Lady Henley and Checkers, chatting amiably as if it were the most natural thing in the world to go around hitting young girls on the head and tying them up.

"What are you going to do with me?" whispered Kitty.

"Oh, you're awake, are you?" said Lady Henley amiably. "Well, I see no harm in letting you know what you're in for, my Lady. In fact I'll kind of enjoy it."

Her stomach gave a faint protesting rumble. "Here, Checkers, got any food in this rat hole?"

Checkers rubbed his fat hands obsequiously. "I have indeed, my Lady. I've got two of the tastiest pigeon pies you ever saw and a spot of mild to wash it down."

"Not cooked by your wife, I hope," asked Lady Henley, forgetting Kitty in the anxiety of the moment.

"No," said the butler reassuringly. "Cooked by a good woman down in the village what is partial to me, you might say."

"Well, stop leering, man, and serve it. I don't suppose she wants her 'last supper.'" Lady Henley grinned at Kitty.

When the food was served she picked up the whole pie in her hands and began to tell Kitty her fate between huge bites.

"I've established with the magistrate that you are in the habit of walking off on your own." She saw Kitty was about to speak and waved the pie at her. "I know what you're thinking. The servants. Not a hope. They're all jailbirds and know when they're well-off, eh, Checkers? They'll all swear blind you went wandering off again. Now where was I? Oh, yes. What's to become of you. Well, something pretty nasty I assure you.

"Checkers here is going to rape you and strangle you and then leave your body in the woods, ain't you, Checkers?"

An unholy smile of glee crossed Lady Henley's face. She put down the pie and stared at Kitty. "You ain't a virgin, are you?"

Kitty blushed painfully and bowed her head. Lady Henley threw back her head and laughed till the tears ran down her fat cheeks. "Well, if that ain't rich! Going to have a bit of fun, eh Checkers?"

The butler sniggered and looked at Kitty, his tongue sliding across his pale lips. Kitty wondered why she didn't die of fright.

Lady Henley finally finished both pies and wiped her mouth with the back of her hand.

"Why do you want to do this to me? Why?" sobbed Kitty.

Lady Henley looked down at her. "Because you're in the way. If you die, I get your mother's money. And I've nearly killed that old bag off with drugs anyway. That's why your mama's been acting so weird. And if I break the news of your rape and murder to her right way, it'll really turn her mind. With any luck she'll commit suicide and save me the trouble. I've been filling her mind up with a lot of filth about your husband so she'll probably think he did it." She patted Kitty on the head. "Well, toodle-oo. Have fun," and with that she lumbered out the door, leaving Kitty and Checkers to stare at each other.

An exhausted Lord Chesworth and Mr. Grange sat in the study of the Thackerays' home and looked at each other in despair.

Albert Grange rubbed his head. "It's as if she's vanished into thin air. She could be anywhere."

Peter sighed and fought against the fatigue that threatened to overwhelm him. "Lady Henley hasn't even got a country place. She sold up over a year ago."

"What and who was she before she married?" asked the detective.

"Before my time," shrugged Peter. "I remember some sort of gossip about her family. Father went mad and shot himself, though it was pretty well hushed up. One of these old county families. No money. But they can trace their line back to the Norman Conquest. There's a *Burke's Peerage* on that table beside you if you want to check up on it."

The detective flicked idly over the pages. "Ah, here we are . . . Henley . . . let's see

. . . married Amelia Pevvy . . . daughter of . . . *what?*"

"What is it?" asked Peter.

"Just that we're absolute fools. Amelia Pevvy of Pevvy Chase — a manor about fourteen miles from where we're sitting," groaned Albert.

"Where's that insufferable ass, Dwight-Hammond?" roared Peter, erupting into the hall.

"What is it?" asked Henry Dwight-Hammond sulkily, emerging from the drawing room with an adoring deb on his arm.

"We need your auto and you're going to drive us," said Peter, disengaging the young man from his partner and pushing him toward the door.

"Here, I say!" expostulated Henry. "You could at least ask nicely."

"We haven't time to say 'pretty please,' you unmitigated ass," roared Peter. "Get in that damned car or I'll tear you apart." His face was white with strain and his eyes blazed with fury.

Henry gave in with bad grace. Albert spread an ordnance survey map on his lap, and with the help of a lantern, navigated the motorcar along the country roads. Twice they took the wrong turning and twice precious minutes were lost while all three raged at one another. At last they turned into the gloomy driveway of Pevvy Chase and there in the light of the car lamps, they could make out a female figure running toward them. Gulping and panting for breath, the terrifled figure of Jenkins looked up at them. She clutched Peter's hand. "Lady Henley took away your missus for a walk today," she gasped. "But she came back alone."

"Get in the car," snapped Peter. They drove up to the entrance of the house in anxiety-ridden silence.

Lady Henley was ensconced in the dining room. She threw down her napkin and glared at the three men. Jenkins had slipped away as quietly as a shadow.

"What do you mean by bursting in here?" demanded Lady Henley.

"Where's my wife?" roared Peter.

Lady Henley gave a fat shrug. "Don't know," she said with magnificent indifference and then glared out of the window. "What are all these policemen doing galumphing about my lawns?"

"I must ask you to come along with me for questioning," said Albert Grange, stepping forward.

Lady Henley's mouth took on a bluish

tinge. "My heart pills," she gasped. She groped in her reticule and extracted a small box, opened it and popped a pill in her mouth. Then she turned to Peter Chesworth with a gloating smile. "By the time you find your little wife, you won't much like what's left of her." Her eyes suddenly bulged and she made several horrible gurglings in the back of her throat.

"She's taken poison!" shouted Grange.

There was an almighty crash and Lady Henley fell across the dining table. She died, as she had lived, with her face in a plate of food.

Albert Grange blew his whistle and several policemen burst into the room. "Round up the servants and find that maid of Lady Henley's."

Cowering, and trembling, Jenkins was at last dragged into the room. Albert Grange motioned to the girl to sit down and poured her a glass of brandy. Lord Chesworth could only wonder at the little detective's patience. "Now, look here, my girl. Drink up your brandy and then tell us if you have any idea where Lady Chesworth might be."

The maid drank the brandy in one gulp and a little color crept into her pallid cheeks. "I followed them a good bit," she said in a whisper. "I'll take you as far as I can." She looked at the dead body of Lady Henley. "At least she can't hurt me any more."

They hurried her out to the motorcar, Peter Chesworth praying under his breath that his wife was still alive.

After Lady Henley had left them, Checkers had started to move toward Kitty, unbuckling the belt of his trousers. Then he hesitated and looked out of the window. "Better wait till dark," he muttered. "You won't be going anywhere, my Lady. You can have a nice afternoon thinking about your death." He bent and slobbered a kiss on her averted face, and with a fat chuckle, took himself off.

For an hour Kitty sat helplessly, feeling sick and dizzy from the blow on her head. She realized it would be no use screaming or they would have gagged her. The rising gale wailed through the trees outside, intensifying the loneliness. Kitty tried to move her wrists but they were so tightly bound that her hands had gone numb. She looked across at the latch on the door. It was a simple iron catch which pushed up to open it. Kitty felt sure that Checkers had not bothered to lock the door.

Twisting her head, she could see that the chair she was bound to was of light cane. She gave a tentative jump and found that she had bumped a little way across the floor.

It was then that terror flooded her as a small ray of hope began to creep into her mind. Without hope, she had been numb. With icy sweat trickling down her body, she tried another jump and got nearer still to the door. Another few bounces and she was under the latch. Muttering a desperate prayer, she lowered her head and banged it on the iron latch. It bounced up and the door swung open on the windy field and the road to freedom.

Her legs trembling and her heart pounding, Kitty bounced out into the field — and stuck fast as the legs of the chair sank into the soft earth.

She would not give up now! Still bound tightly to the chair, she fell to the ground and started to roll to the hedge at the edge of the field. Over and over, her face digging into the soft ground, straining every muscle, she finally rolled into a ditch and stared up at the storm-torn sky.

Kitty turned over on her side and tried to control the terrible trembling that racked her body from head to foot. Her eye caught the dull gleam of a rusty scythe blade a few yards from where she lay. She wrenched herself over and over, her face stung by long nettles, until she was lying against it. It took her fifteen minutes of panting and straining, until she got her wrists into position against the dull blade. She could only move them a little way up and down the scythe. A crow perched on the edge of the broken scythe handle and watched her every move like a bird of ill-omen. The strands suddenly parted all at once and she bit her lip until the blood came to stifle the cry of pain which rose to her lips as the feeling began to return to her hands. Precious minutes were spent massaging them until she was finally able to free her feet.

Kitty stumbled erect and looked around, gathering her strength for a plunge into the woods. Then at the far corner of the field she saw Checkers returning. She would crouch down in the ditch until he had gone into the cottage and then make her escape.

But before she knew what was happening Kitty found herself striding to meet Checkers with the scythe in her hand. Through a red mist of rage she saw his start of surprise and heard his complacent chuckle.

"So Kitty has claws," said Checkers advancing on her. "Good. I likes them with a bit of fight in 'em." He lumbered towards her, still laughing and chuckling.

In one brief, lucid flash before the red mist closed upon her again, Kitty thought with surprise, "Now I know what a cornered rat feels like."

She sidestepped Checkers as he reached for the scythe and swiped him across the legs. He shrieked with pain and bent to clutch his injured legs when Kitty raised the blunt edge of the scythe and brought it down on his bald head, terror and rage lending her twice the strength. Checkers fell and lay still.

Kitty turned and ran out into the lane, headlong into the gloom and the green tunnels. Night had fallen and still she ran, choking and sobbing for breath.

The ground about her seemed to heave with the increasing violence of the storm, although she was protected from its full force by the height of the hedges on either side of the road.

She ran on around a corner of the lane and found herself blinded by a dazzling light in the middle of the road and started to scramble up the steep bank to safety. The sound of her name being shouted by several people finally penetrated Kitty's fear and she stopped in her flight and slowly turned. The first person she saw was Mr. Albert Grange and with a sob of relief, she threw herself into his arms.

"Now, then, now then," said the detective. "You're all right now. Everything's going to be all right. Here's your husband."

Kitty looked over his shoulder into Peter Chesworth's face and collapsed, unconscious, into the detective's arms.

Chapter Ten

Peter Chesworth was in the country and his wife was in town. "This could go on forever," he sighed to himself.

Autumn was sending its red and gold colors sweeping through the woods around Reamington Hall. Smoke rose lazily into the clear air from the gardener's bonfire, a bumper harvest had been brought in, and fires crackled merrily in all the rooms of the Hall to disperse the October chill.

Kitty had been taken to the Thackerays' home at Cowes to recover from her fright and exhaustion. On the second day she had contracted pneumonia and for two weeks she hung between life and death, as her husband paced outside her room upstairs, and downstairs, the Thackerays grumbled about the enforced sort of semimourning which hung over their home. They blamed it all on Kitty's origins. The middle classes, as everyone knew, were notorious wet blankets.

Finally, little by little, Kitty began to recover her strength as summer fled from the countryside and the yachts were hauled up for repairs. Chrysanthemums blazed in the rooms instead of roses. The Indian-summer sun dawned and set and still Kitty would not see her husband.

Lady Mainwaring tried to reason with her but Kitty only began to sob in a weak way and shake her head.

The shock of the final attempt on her life had left Kitty nervous and jumpy and unwilling to face anyone who had hurt or humiliated her in the slightest. Henry Dwight-Hammond and Cyril Lawton had been asked to leave a long time ago, for the very sight of either of them sent Kitty into a fever. The Thackerays had finally departed for Rooks Neuk, leaving Kitty and Lady Mainwaring alone with a skeleton staff.

At last Emily Mainwaring felt that she would scream with boredom from the daily diet of gentle walks, light meals, and lengthy silences. She at last confronted Kitty with the sharp remark, "I think you're turning into a spoiled brat!"

Kitty looked at her with tears forming in her eyes.

"Oh, don't start blubbering again," snapped Lady Mainwaring. "I'm tired to death of being stuck down here and I think you're now well enough to think about someone other than yourself. So there it is, harsh as it may be. I'm bored and your husband is at Reamington Hall, worrying himself to death about you."

Kitty shifted uneasily and dried her eyes. "I'm sorry, Emily. I don't seem to have much spirit left. You're right. Let's go back to London."

"I didn't say anything about London. *I'm* going to London. *You're* going to Reamington Hall."

"Oh, not yet. Please Emily," begged Kitty. "Let me stay with you for a little bit."

"Oh, well," shrugged Emily. "I may as well take you home with me. But remember, I'm a social animal. I like my theaters and parties and my house full of people."

Kitty suddenly smiled for the first time in weeks. "I feel better already. I think I could even look forward to a party."

"That's more like it," said Emily. "Now, don't you feel strong enough and curious enough to know the outcome of all the trouble?"

Kitty took a deep breath and nodded. Emily Mainwaring sat back and began her story.

"First of all, Grange and a squad of policemen went up the road and found Checkers unconscious in the field. Someone had hit him with a scythe. . . . Good God . . . was that you?

"Anyway, they discovered he has a record of assault and violence as long as your arm. The rest of the servants at Pevvy Chase also had pretty rotten records, except for Jenkins. Lady Henley took poison before she could be charged with anything so that's good riddance to bad rubbish. Your mother was sent to the hospital suffering from an overdose of fairly complicated drugs administered by Euphemia Henley.

"Well, the long and the short of it is, your mama's her usual horrible self — oops, sorry — and has plunged into her husband's old business and seems in a fair way to be trebling her fortune. She says the aristocracy are the scum of the earth and prefers to associate with merchants' wives.

"Mr. Grange got promoted to Chief Detective-Inspector although he feels the honor was given to him not because he solved the case but because he appears to be on first name terms with your husband . . . which is a very cynical way of looking at it, but probably true.

"Your husband went back to work on his beloved estate after about your hundredth refusal to see him. Let me see, what else? Oh yes, the Dwight-Hammond sisters discovered that one of their maids had put the snakes in the bed. A man answering Checkers' description had told her it was just a bit of a joke and that they were harmless grass snakes. Needless to say, she got well paid for doing it. She broke down and confessed when she read about your adventures in the papers. And it was Checkers who tried to kill you by sawing off the balcony.

"So that's that. Let's get packed and get out of this dead-alive hole."

The house in Regents Park looked the same but did not feel the same. Early morning frost had blackened the remaining flowers and a mist rose from the canal, but it was Lady Mainwaring's constant entertaining which made the difference. Kitty felt as though she was living in the middle of an eternal house party and after describing her ordeal for the fifteenth time to yet another party of guests, she began to feel that the whole thing had been a dream.

An odd feeling of belonging nowhere,

neither to house nor class, assailed her. As the nights drew on, she began to think sentimentally about the house in Hampstead, forgetting the penny-pinching and the chill rooms.

Hetty! She had forgotten all about Hetty. Perhaps if she could stay with her old friend in Hampstead for a bit, she could get her bearings again. She did not want to think about her husband. Kitty felt, unfairly, that most of her trouble was Peter's fault. She could not remember his kindness and endearments; only the mocking aristocrat of her wedding night who said he had only married her for her money.

But Kitty did not realize how much she had changed. Used to the type of society who called in for a visit at a country house and then stayed for weeks, she never dreamt of sending Hetty a message. Packing her trunks and calling for the carriage, Kitty could only see the rosy picture in her mind of sitting in front of the fire with Hetty and feeling at home.

It was late afternoon by the time she was ready to leave. Lady Mainwaring had not returned from her calls so Kitty scribbled a note of explanation and left it on the hall table.

As she was getting into the carriage, she

felt a gentle touch on her arm and found herself staring down into the thin, frightened face of Jenkins, the maid.

"Please, my Lady," begged Jenkins. "Just a little money, for the love of God. I can't find work anywhere."

Kitty felt her face burning with guilt. Emily was right. She had thought of no one but berself. She told the coachman to wait and led the shivering maid into the house and rang for the housekeeper. "This is Jenkins who has just been employed as my personal maid."

The housekeeper looked at the shabby girl without her face moving a muscle. Lady Mainwaring trained her servants well.

"Please see that she is supplied with the necessary clothes and uniforms," Kitty went on. "I really must leave. The carriage is waiting." Jenkins looked downcast and Kitty cursed herself for her own selfishness. "Come upstairs with me a minute, Jenkins, and I will explain your duties."

Once in her bedroom, Kitty turned to the maid. "Why didn't you get in touch with me sooner, Jenkins?"

Jenkins bowed her head. "The police found out about my prison record so no one would let me near you."

Kitty fumbled in her reticule and found her purse. "Here's some money, Jenkins, just to get some odds and ends. I shall probably be away for only a few days."

Jenkins's face lit up with a radiant smile. "I'll serve you to the end of my days, my Lady. You see if I don't."

"Nonsense!" said Kitty. "I should hope you will get married soon. All young girls should have a husband," she added lightly and then bit her lip as a picture of her own husband came into her mind. But she forced herself to talk patiently and calmly to the girl about her duties, not realizing that by this very action, Kitty Harrison was now the Baroness Reamington in more than just title. Then having assured herself that Jenkins would be taken care of until her return, she ran lightly down the stairs and told the coachman to drive to Hampstead.

How jolly and familiar everything looked! How the lights sparkled from Carson's bakery. How beautiful and familiar her beloved Heath looked, stretched out peacefully under the London twilight.

But at the Carsons' home in Gospel Oak, Kitty received her first setback. Hetty was married, explained a much-flustered Mrs. Carson. Yes, indeed. And to John

Stokes. And what was even more wonderful, they had bought Kitty's old home just up the hill. Kitty's face fell. She had not envisaged any men in the picture.

After she had left Mrs. Carson, Kitty directed the carriage to her old home and then stood for a minute by the gate. From the outside it did not seem to have changed a bit.

The door flew open and Hetty bounced out. "Kitty! I saw the carriage arriving and —" She broke off as she saw the coachman unstrapping Kitty's trunk from the back of the carriage.

"I came to stay for a little," blurted out Kitty. "I didn't know you were married, Hetty. If it's at all inconvenient, I'll leave."

"Not at all," burbled Hetty, excited at the prospect of having a notorious society lady under her roof. "John will be delighted. You were in all the papers. It was ever so exciting. Wait till the neighbors learn who's come to stay!"

Hetty chattered on, her ringlets bobbing with their familiar bounce. The house looked much the same inside, as Mrs. Harrison had sold the furniture along with it. But at least it was now warm. John Stokes got to his feet when they came into the parlor. His clothes looked even tighter than before.

"Why, Kitty," he exclaimed, getting to his feet. "Well, who would have guessed you'd turn out to be such a looker." He kissed her on the cheek with unnecessary warmth.

"Now," said Hetty, excitedly, "I'll tell the maid to get your old room ready and you can tell us all about your adventures."

Kitty looked nervously at John Stokes. She had planned to tell Hetty all about it when they were alone together. But John was leaning forward from his armchair, as eager as his wife.

So instead of the delicious burst of confidences she had planned, Kitty told her story for the umpteenth time in a tired, flat voice. Hetty clapped her hands and oohed and aahed as if Kitty had become more of a sideshow at a carnival than a friend.

By the time the pair of them let her go and she wearily climbed the familiar stairs to bed, Kitty felt very lost and tired.

Everything looked familiar but did not *feel* familiar. She had returned to her own class and surroundings. Why then was the feeling of homelessness stronger than ever? She stood at the window for a long time looking out across the Heath that was spread out under a large autumn moon.

The following two days were as bad as being at Lady Mainwaring's. Hetty filled the house with her friends from morning till night and on one occasion when she had pleaded a headache, Hetty had cried so much and been so disappointed that she had felt obliged to join the company.

After one such day when she had escaped to her room, Hetty followed her.

"I'm surprised that your clothes are so simple, Kitty," pouted Hetty. "I declare I'm better dressed than you are." She pirouetted in front of Kitty in a creation that was so gored and hemmed and herringboned and tucked and rucked that she had achieved the rare distinction of making tweed look frivolous.

"And haven't you any jewels?" said Hetty. "A tiara or some such thing?"

"Come now," smiled Kitty. "I would only wear a tiara to a very grand ball."

Hetty stamped her foot. "There you go! Implying that we aren't good enough for you."

Kitty saw a chance for the confidential talk. "Of course I don't think you're not good enough for me. It's just that I'm worried about my husband."

Hetty's wide blue eyes gleamed and her voice dropped to a whisper. "Is he going to divorce you?"

"No," said Kitty faintly. "Of course not."

"Well, it looks very odd to me," said Hetty, sitting down in a chair and kicking off her shoes. "Take John and me. We're always together and ever so lovey-dovey. Anyone would think you had been married for years."

Kitty sat forward, anxious to explain. "It's not that, Hetty. It's just that our marriage got off to a bad start. . . ."

"I'll say it did," said Hetty rudely. "Him and that Mrs. Jackson. Ought to be ashamed of himself. We hear the society gossip even out here in Hampstead, you know. Is he with her now?"

Kitty raised her hands to her face and stared at Hetty. "Of course not! Of course not! After what she tried to do to me?"

"What did she try to do?" asked Hetty eagerly.

Kitty bit her lip in confusion. She remembered that Mrs. Jackson's attempt on her life had been hushed up. "Well, she was always trying to take him away from me," amended Kitty.

"Is that all," said Hetty, disappointed. "I'd just like to see someone try to take my

John away from me."

"But it's not the same . . ." began Kitty.

"Oh, so it's all different in high society, is it?" sneered Hetty.

The conversation was not going at all the way Kitty wanted it. In fact it was heading for disaster. Without being aware of it she reverted to one of Hetty's ruses and put her arms around the angry girl.

"Now, Hetty, you know I'm your friend. I wouldn't dream of saying anything to hurt you."

Much mollified, Hetty, however, saw that Kitty was in a vulnerable state and was quick to turn it to her advantage.

"You know, dear Kitty, me and John would like you to stay ever so long. But what with paying the servants and the extra entertaining, we're having to pinch pennies. . . ."

Kitty blushed in confusion. "I never thought about money. I'll arrange some for you tomorrow."

"Tomorrow's Sunday," pointed out Hetty quickly.

"Well, Monday then," said poor Kitty, feeling thoroughly embarrassed. But Hetty was not. "Ta muchly," she said, dropping a kiss on the top of Kitty's head as she prepared to leave. "You mustn't mind me talking about money, but I've always prided myself on being frank and honest." Picking up her shoes, she left the room without having shown one ounce of concern over Kitty's obvious worry about her husband.

Kitty got ready for church the next morning, fighting against a growing feeling of dislike for her hostess. All her old surroundings seemed to have done for her was to reduce her to the former Kitty Harrison, quiet, shy, and unhappy, without any of the feelings of security and comfort she had expected.

The morning was gray and foggy. The Indian summer had fled and turned the world over to winter. Wreaths of chilly, throat-catching fog shrouded the roads and lanes of Hampstead and snaked their way through the branches of the trees on the Heath. This visit to church was to be the culmination of Hetty's social triumph and she meant to make the most of it.

Before they left the house Hetty drew Kitty aside, out of earshot of her husband. "Now, I don't want any of your die-away airs, Kitty," said Hetty sharply, surveying her subdued friend. "Lady Worthing will be in church and she will want to talk to you but she will try and cut me. You're not to let her, mind that! You're to introduce me properly — in a loud voice."

"Yes, Hetty," said Kitty faintly. She had nearly said, "Yes, Mama!" as Hetty sounded so like her mother. With an unreal feeling of having stepped back in time, Kitty left the house in Hetty's wake. "Cheer up, Kitty," said John Stokes, putting an arm around her and squeezing her waist. "The missus gets a bit carried away." Kitty shrank from him in distaste and he responded with an offended glare and was overly affectionate to his wife all the way to the church.

Still in a dream Kitty followed the Stokeses into their pew. There was Lady Worthing as of old, attired in an unsuitable hat of garden-party lace which the fog had already soiled at the edge. Her eyes bulged when she saw Kitty and the glass eyes of the little furry animals around her neck seemed to bulge in sympathy. Fog filtered into the church and hung in long, smoky bars over the pulpit where the Reverend James Ponsonby-Smythe again recited the tale of who begat whom. Kitty's mind wandered away from the Bible readings to the time before her marriage.

How funny, she thought. I feel that if I turned my head I would see him standing at the back of the church. Then, in a great painful wave, the memories came tumbling one after another into her mind. The way he smiled, the mocking look in his gray eyes when he was amused, the feel of his hands on her body . . . his kiss. Slowly, she turned around and looked toward the back of the church.

No one. Only a sooty angel above the entrance, staring at her impassively through the thickening fog.

Oh, God, no one. What on earth was she doing here in Hampstead? She should be with her husband. She should be home. What an unutterable fool she had been. To have the world and more and to throw it all away, moping around Hampstead with Hetty. Hetty, who did not care one little bit for her. Hetty, who would have shown her the door if Kitty had not been a Baroness. Kitty put her gloved hand up to her flushed cheeks. She must have been mad, out of her mind. God! God! What if he wouldn't take her back?

Kitty Harrison had entered the church, but as the last sonorous "amen" sounded, the Baroness Reamington got to her feet and marched to the door.

Lady Worthing was waiting for her on the porch. "My dear, Lady Chesworth," she positively simpered. "So nice to have you back among us."

"She's staying with me," said Hetty fiercely.

Stumbling slightly on her two-and-seven-eighths-of-an-inch heels, Hetty pushed herself in front of Kitty. "Aren't you going to introduce me, Kitty dear?" said Hetty, pinching her friend's arm. Kitty politely made the introduction which Lady Worthing ignored. She drew Kitty's arm through her own and said in a loud voice, "Really, my dear Lady Chesworth, I should have thought you would have cut your connections with tradespeople."

"Not at all," said the Baroness sweetly. "I am not like my mother, Lady Worthing. I should never dream of cutting you just because your money comes from trade."

Hetty sniggered with delight and to Kitty's horror, Lady Worthing's eyes filled with hurt tears. "That's telling her, Kitty," crowed Hetty triumphantly. But to her annoyance, Kitty smiled at Lady Worthing and said in a voice loud enough to carry to the ears of the listening congregation, "I would be very honored if you would call on me when I am next in town. I plan to start entertaining and I am sure you would like your daughters to meet suitable beaux."

Lady Worthing gave her a look of pure gratitude and muttered gruffly that she would be delighted. Kitty then set off down the hill at a great pace with Hetty stumbling furiously after her.

"What on earth were you doing — being nice to that old bitch?" raged Hetty.

Kitty could hardly explain it to herself. She only knew that she had suddenly realized that Lady Worthing was a lonely, silly old woman with nothing but her position as Princess of Hampstead to keep her going. She had felt sorry for her. Still, Kitty could not help understanding Hetty's rage a little. There had been no need for her to be *so* kind.

Instead of replying to Hetty's question, Kitty slowed her walk and stated that she would be leaving London for the country. Hetty shrugged. "We *were* beginning to wonder when you were going to leave. You will remember the money you promised, won't you, Kitty, *dear?*"

"Of course," said Kitty sharply. "Perhaps as a last favor you could ask your maid to pack for me. I'm going for a walk." And oblivious of John Stokes's cry of "What! In this weather?" she left the road and plunged into the Heath, walking straight in front of her until the sounds of the home-going congregation had faded behind her. "What on earth had prompted me to go and stay with Hetty?" she thought savagely.

"What on earth prompted her to go and stay with Hetty?" Lord Peter Chesworth stared at Lady Mainwaring in surprise. "Don't ask me," she snapped. "How should I know? *Nostalgie de la boue* or something like that. She's been pretty shaken-up by the whole business, of course.

"I am disappointed," she went on. "I got so interested in that girl but I suppose I fancied myself a bit of a Pygmalion and got carried away. Kitty seemed to be becoming so sure of herself and sophisticated and then — bam! She was weeping and sniveling."

"Don't be so damned cruel," said Peter waspishly. "She's been through a lot. Do you think there's any chance of her coming back to me?"

Emily Mainwaring looked at him and took a deep breath. "Not if you mope around here, there isn't. For God's sake man, who would ever have thought that

Peter Chesworth would need instruction where women are concerned. Forget she's your wife. Go and kiss her and drag her back by the hair. If you don't, she'll potter the rest of her life away, dithering from home to home. To be crude — go and have a try at that long-preserved virginity."

Peter Chesworth suddenly grinned. "What a horrible woman you are to be sure. But I'll try anything. Although I hope I can find her in this weather."

His carriage crawled its way through the yellow fog in the direction of Hampstead. When he reached Gospel Oak, there was a delay while Mrs. Carson gave him instructions on how to get to her daughter's home.

Then there was a very ruffled and petulant Hetty to deal with, when he finally found the right address. At last she volunteered that Kitty had gone walking on the Heath and if my Lord asked her opinion, his wife had gone off her head.

No, "my Lord" hadn't asked her opinion and didn't want it either. Peter Chesworth slammed his way out of Hetty's home, leaving her to take her temper out on her husband. John Stokes thought she was angry because he had put his arm around Kitty and assumed Kitty had complained to his wife. "She's such an attractive little thing," pleaded John. "I couldn't resist giving her a bit of a cuddle."

Hetty naturally demanded a full explanation and having got it, promptly went into strong hysterics and would have gone on all afternoon, if John Stokes had not, with an unexpected turn of strength, slapped her across the face with the full force of his pudgy hand.

Kitty sat on a bench on a rise in the middle of the Heath and stared dismally at a wall of fog a few inches in front of her face. In fact, it was all so miserable she felt almost glad. She could not be expected to take any action in a fog like this — any action, that is, like going back and facing the one-time friend she now detested. So although Kitty knew every inch of the Heath and could easily have picked her way to the road, she stayed where she was, looking at her feet and listening to the sound of water dripping from the trees all around her.

Kitty had often sat on this bench before and could remember the view on a summer's day when the Heath seemed to roll from beneath one's feet all the way down to the spires of London Town. How she used to sit and dream that the church spires of Central London were in fact the towers of Camelot and that if she sat very still and waited long enough, she would see her knight riding up the hill toward her.

She heaved a great sigh that moved the fog slightly in front of her face and, as if in mischievous reply, a small breath of wind rippled through the fog sending it streaming in ribbons across the grass. Then the heavy silence fell again. But the little breeze returned with his playmates and suddenly, all about her, the thick fog started moving and shifting and swirling, making changing shapes and figures dance through the trees like so many ghosts. Mrs. Barlowe-Smellie slid behind a birch with a teacup in her hands, Lady Henley loomed up and dispersed in fragments and Checkers and the housekeeper from Pevvy Chase did a mad sarabande in the bushes. Now she could see several yards in front of her and somewhere high above London the sun must have been shining for the fog began to change to a light golden yellow.

Then the little breeze seemed to scamper away leaving a few moments of stillness and quiet until with a great whoo-oo-oo-sh, the east wind swept across the expanse of the Heath like some great bustling mother looking for her naughty children.

The huge bank of fog rolled away, the sun shone down bravely on the sparkling grass and there, far away, were the spires of Kitty's Camelot. And walking slowly up the Heath towards her came her husband.

Kitty slowly got to her feet and walked forward. Both of them were desperately rehearsing in their minds what they would say and do. They had nearly reached each other when a great gust of wind swirled a thick cloud of dead leaves around them. Kitty stumbled and fell down the hill into his arms. Peter collapsed under her weight and they both burst out laughing and giggling as they rolled over and over to the bottom of the hill, Peter Chesworth smothering his wife's face in kisses. At last, they came to a stop and sat up, both of them covered in grass stains and wet leaves and twigs. Neither one had said a word to the other. Neither had uttered any of the well-rehearsed speech in mind.

Slowly, Peter reached out his long fingers and took his wife's chin in his hand. What an infinity of sky, sun, turning leaves, and glittering grass before his lips met hers.

The sky faded to a deep blue barred with long, thin, crimson and yellow clouds be-

fore the Baron and the Baroness left the
Heath. The evening star shone out and
one by one the twinkling lights of nighttime London began to reflect its beauty.
Blissfully unaware of the curious stares of
passing stragglers, the couple stopped occasionally to kiss, to laugh and, like all
lovers the world over, to "do you remember when. . . ."

Kitty's trunk was corded ready on the
step and the Baroness was told by the terrified little maid that her mistress was "not
at home."

Hetty twitched the lace curtains as the
couple climbed dreamily into the carriage
and sank into a long embrace.

"Just look at that, John! Behaving in that
disgraceful way. And on a Sunday too! And
they're all mud and leaves all over. You
wouldn't catch me behaving like that."

Her husband said nothing, but he
watched the carriage with a wistful expression on his chubby face until it had turned
the corner and disappeared from view.

Chapter Eleven

A long wailing scream echoed along the corridor from the rooms allocated to the Hon. Jeremy and Mrs. Thackeray. "Good heavens!" exclaimed Peter Chesworth, putting down his newspaper. He looked across at his wife who was supervising the trimming of the tree. "Don't tell me you put something in their bed!"

"Holly. A great big bunch of prickly holly, complete with berries," said Kitty. "Very seasonal."

It was Christmas at Reamington Hall and Kitty was enjoying her first house party. The Thackerays had been the first to arrive and had retired to their rooms for an afternoon nap.

Colonel Barlowe-Smellie was the next arrival, followed by his twittering wife and apprehensive son, Percy. Percy had not forgotten Kitty's calling him a rude young man and was obviously determined to be on his best behavior. Dropping various wraps and Christmas parcels, Mrs. Barlowe-Smellie rushed forward to kiss

Kitty while her husband's grumbled monologue ran in and out of her broken sentences.

"So kind . . ." said Mrs. Barlowe-Smellie looking around the decorated room with pleasure ". . . love Christmas . . . Santa Claus . . . 'Hark the Herald Angels' . . . holly, mistletoe . . . but so insanitary . . . kissing just anyone . . . butler last year . . . Madeira . . . embarrassing . . . tut . . ." — "Load of pagan rubbish, what?" said the colonel — ". . . pretty Kitty . . . such a difference . . . murder . . . terrible experience . . . tut . . ." — "Never liked that fat old woman," said the colonel — ". . . and Veronica Jackson married . . ." — "Tart! Got a whiskey and soda?" asked the colonel.

"What?" exclaimed Kitty and Peter together.

"What's wrong with wanting a whiskey and soda in this weather?" grumped the colonel angrily. "Shouldn't even have to ask, what!" His face was turning an alarming color so Kitty and Peter hastened to reassure him that their surprise was only at the news of Veronica Jackson's marriage. "Tell us about it," they begged Mrs. Barlowe-Smellie.

Mrs. Barlowe-Smellie turned positively pink with pleasure. Because of her fragmented manner of speaking, people rarely listened to her let alone asked her to tell a whole story. She settled herself beside the fire, took a deep breath, and began.

By filling in the gaps Kitty pieced together that Veronica had gone to Baden-Baden after being cleared of the other attempts on Kitty's life. She had fallen in love with a handsome young man, a Count Von Richelstag. As he had seemed to be very wealthy, she had given him to understand that she was a very rich woman. Only after they were married, did Veronica find out that her Count was virtually penniless and had only married her for her supposed money. The last report was that they were ensconced on his crumbling estate in Saxony, making life hell for each other.

"Nemesis . . ." fluttered Mrs. Barlowe-Smellie, ". . . not often people like that get their deserts . . . very democratic!"

The last remark referred not to the unfortunate Veronica and her husband, but to the arrival of Albert Grange and his wife.

"Beginning to snow," announced Albert, brushing his bowler and handing it to the butler. "Got a bit of a shock down the road. Chap rushed out of a cottage and nearly fell under the wheels. Kept hanging on to me and telling me to repent."

Peter sighed, "That's Bob Pugsley, one of the estate workers. He lost his addiction to drink and dogs and joined some peculiar religious sect. But he does the work of about five men. It was Mrs. Pugsley who turned out to miss the joys of London the most. She packed up a month ago and went back to Camden Town. Pugsley doesn't mind. He sends her money regularly along with a barrowload of religious tracts."

Lady Mainwaring was the next to arrive, bringing Kitty news of her old friend Hetty. "She was so threatening and hysterical, I had to threaten *her* with the police," said Emily. "I really don't know why people like snow at Christmas. So wet and cold and nasty."

"What on earth happened to Hetty?" exclaimed Kitty. "And why was she threatening you?"

Emily spread her fingers out to the blaze of the wood fire. "Get me a drink and I'll tell you all. Thank you Peter. Now, where was I? Oh, yes. Hetty. She had been to your town house looking for you and she was in a terrible state. Her husband had run away to Brighton with one of the girls from the shop and, in some peculiar way, Hetty wanted to blame it all on you. She said you had infected her husband's mind with your loose, aristocratic life-style. The long and the short of it is I told her not to talk such twaddle and to take herself off and she tried to scratch my face. *That* was when I threatened her with the police."

"Poor Hetty," said Kitty.

"Poor nothing," sniffed Emily. "She's a thoroughly nasty little girl."

After the guests had warmed themselves, Kitty rang for the housekeeper to show them to their rooms and went to join her husband by the window.

The snow whirled and danced across the lawns, swirling and turning among the old trees; one minute falling as gently as on a Christmas card and the next blowing in great white sheets, blotting everything from view.

Peter Chesworth slowly took his wife in his arms and closed his eyes, conscious of nothing but the lips beneath his and the slim body against his.

"Oh dear," twittered Mrs. Barlowe-Smellie from the doorway, ". . . very moving . . . to think . . . colonel and myself . . . so long ago . . . India . . . heat and flies . . . but babies . . . must set up your nursery

. . good nanny . . . so important . . . dear me . . . romantic . . . very romantic."

"What y' mumbling about now?" said her husband joining her in the doorway.

"Oh, go back to your whiskey and shut up," said Mrs. Barlowe-Smellie, clearly and distinctly.

The employees of Thorndike Press hope you have enjoyed this Large Print book. All our Thorndike and Wheeler Large Print titles are designed for easy reading, and all our books are made to last. Other Thorndike Press Large Print books are available at your library, through selected bookstores, or directly from us.

For information about titles, please call:

(800) 223-1244

or visit our Web site at:

www.gale.com/thorndike
www.gale.com/wheeler

To share your comments, please write:

Publisher
Thorndike Press
295 Kennedy Memorial Drive
Waterville, ME   04901